How Great Thou Art

A Black Boy's Depression-Era Success Story

Walter H. Richardson

authorHOUSE®

AuthorHouse™
1663 Liberty Drive, Suite 200
Bloomington, IN 47403
www.authorhouse.com
Phone: 1-800-839-8640

First published by AuthorHouse 11/5/2008

ISBN: 978-1-4343-8393-8 (e)
ISBN: 978-1-4343-8392-1 (sc)
ISBN: 978-1-4389-0951-6 (hc)

Library of Congress Control Number: 2008904276

Printed in the United States of America
Bloomington, Indiana

This book is printed on acid-free paper.

Acknowledgments

It is with great joy that I recognize those who inspired me to share my memoirs. There were times when I felt just talking about my life's experience was sufficient. Then after hearing it over and over that I should write those events for others to read, especially the generations of Richardsons following me, I finally gave in.

I am extremely grateful to Helen, my lovely wife of 54 years, who walked this journey with me. I depended upon her to say whether I should share this event or not. The children all agreed that my story was unique, and they are very proud of the way I controlled unpleasant circumstances. My greatest inspiration has come from Walter II, who is simply wonderful. He encouraged me to share my experiences with others outside of the family so as to help them to find hope when things were not always going well. Wayne, a great motivator, followed in my footsteps as a career military professional. I relied upon him during heavy crises when he was always able to provide an answer plus a guiding light to travel on. Lillie, truly a deeply inspiring person, strongly encouraged me to tell my story. Carmen, most energetic, supported me from the beginning. As a professional school teacher, she knew my story would help young people to take charge of their behavior and to succeed. Henri, a great singer and entertainer, asked that I tell my story because there were so many times he watched me perform on stage. Donna, an executive administrator, helped tremendously by reading and editing my work. William, likewise a professional sales representative with a major pharmaceutical company, was instrumental in reading my work and telling me where I should place more emphasis. Carl, a professor of Fine Arts at a Community College, put together the illustrations. There are a host of others to whom I am extremely grateful for supporting this project.

I owe a great deal of my achievements to the United States Air Force, its officers and my fellow airmen and the civilians I worked and lived with for over 30 years. The Air Force provided me with many challenges. Those challenges were always an opportunity to excel.

A tremendous amount of encouragement came from my dear adopted sister, Juanita Sanks, who was always available to listen and give spiritual advice.

I would be remiss if I failed to acknowledge Michael Bradley, who continuously insisted that I put my life's experiences in writing to help others to develop faith, hope, and to love others as they should love themselves. Likewise, I am grateful to Wayne and Connie Brown for giving me a journal each year to record significant events of my life.

I want to thank everyone who inspired me to write my memoirs. Names will appear throughout the book that deserve recognition as a friend, co-worker, supervisor, military leader, and associate. I am extremely grateful for your friendship and moral support.

Last but not least, I thank my Father, God, for giving me such an exciting assignment during this temporary assignment on planet Earth.

Dedication to Helen, My Lovely Wife, My Life

**THE BEGINNING - Helen's Junior College
photo – her first gift to me.**

Contents

Prologue

The title of my memoirs suggests the power of love springing up from the greatness and goodness of God.

I was inspired to share my life story with others, particularly my grandchildren, and with generations to come, to record what I learned very early in life: GOD IS NOT BIASED, he creates everyone in His image and claims us all as His children.

Equipped with this knowledge of God's love (in a real sense) and developing over time a positive spiritual attitude, I grew up with a mindset disregarding racial prejudices, social rejections and countless unjust situations. I did this all for the love of God, our true Father.

Being born and growing up in the South during the advent of the Depression, I was in a fertile environment to generate and perpetuate racial bitterness. Fortunately, that bitterness did not develop in me because it was discouraged by a devout Christian mother, as well as an elementary teacher and a Sunday school leader, all of whom had suffered hardships from both sides – Negroes and Whites as well.

This instilled in me the initiative to achieve success in spite of obstacles and to stay focused on the only true love and source of justice which exist in the world and which can be found only in God, my true FATHER.

Sharing my life story may remind you of stages in your life regardless of your age, culture or gender. This story also seeks to enlighten and encourage all people to strive for and achieve a lasting relationship with

God and to have faith that will deliver you from all evil. I did it and it worked for me. "My God, How Great Thou Art."

Walter Harold Richardson

Introduction:
Filling the Hole in His Soul

WALTER H. RICHARDSON is born at high noon on February 12, 1929 – that inauspicious year when the Great Depression will soon begin to rage and raze, pillage, and savage a defenseless country.

For most folks, this period of raw, debilitating austerity will last until World War II but, for Walter and his family, it will persist perniciously way beyond that point, as it will for most people of color.

Born to an unwed mother, the Boy from Jackson Street feels abandoned when his father forsakes all responsibility for any of his needs – physical AND emotional – leaving a big bad hole in his good little soul. As balm for his festering wound, his devout and clever mother convinces him that his REAL daddy is his "Father in Heaven."

Economic and spousal deficiencies notwithstanding, Miss Lilly refuses to bend to the clouds, winds and storms of ubiquitous adversity; her three children become her sole reason for suffering, survival and ultimate success. As is often the case for an only son, Walter unquestionably is the apple of his mother's eye, the zenith of her life, the promise for posterity. The Boy from Jackson Street responds in kind by living his whole life in a quest and struggle to excel, keeping always "his nose clean," no matter what slights, insults and assaults are hurled at him...all in repayment for Mom's wise counsel, unbounded love and – some would say – near adoration of this, her child prodigy.

Together, Miss Lilly and her Depression Baby will endure and prevail over the harsh cruelties and illogical absurdities of Jim Crow segregation, as if to say: <u>A peaceful mountain is surely worth climbing after a cascading river has been forded</u>. "Don't cry for me as long as I have my health," she would muse.

Walter Richardson cries easily, frequently and unapologetically, perhaps owing to the latent effects of that ole hole in his soul which has healed but is covered over with layers of encrusted scar tissue. More likely, he weeps in appreciation for piles and piles of blessings from "DAD."

What has been wrought for Walter by Miss Lilly's bargain with her responsive Maker? How about an angel for a wife? Eight holy, healthy, happy children, all college-educated and upright people. Don't forget nine grandchildren. Add outstanding achievements in military, organizational, business and (above all) religious spheres, many of which have never before been attained by a black man.

This James Earle Jones look-alike, sound-alike is a happy man, a gracious, generous, spiritual, talented man who sings his way through life – literally and figuratively – like it is all preordained. "Well . . . isn't it?" he would surely josh.

As this is being written, a front-page, above-the-fold article in the regional daily is touting Richardson's deft handling of construction of a veterans' medical facility – which, of all things, is running <u>under</u> budget and <u>ahead</u> of time . . . and a federal contract no less.

When congratulated for this oxymoronic development, the Boy from Jackson Street accepts proudly but modestly, all the while giving credit to YOU KNOW WHO.

Most readers will know that the title for this book is garnered from a powerful hymn which pays tribute to Walter's REAL FATHER IN HEAVEN – a song with which he can rattle the rafters in perfect key, tone and pitch, powerfully proclaiming, "HOW GREAT THOU ART!"

And why not?

M. Jude Saints

Lilly Richardson:
Star in the Tom Black Line

My Mom will be mentioned frequently during the telling of my life's story. Considered a pillar of strength and undying faith by yours truly and others who knew her, she undoubtedly provided the spiritual leadership which helped me to achieve the incredibly good things of my life.

Just to describe her for posterity brings about an uplifting feeling that is simply indescribable, but to share her interests along with her tireless Christian endeavors is a joy and privilege without equal.

Lilly was born November 2, 1903 in Jackson, Mississippi and died on my birthday, February 12, 1981 in Pensacola, Florida at the age of 78. (As this is being written, I am 78.)

A very attractive lady, she was five feet, four inches tall, had a rich "café-au-lait" complexion and beautifully-shaped, near-perfect brown eyes.

She wore a lovely, subdued but endearing smile and, above all, had a terrific sense of humor. O God, she really loved to make people laugh. That special gift helped her cope with an avalanche of unfortunate situations in her early life, which she refused to discuss.

Her dad, Leslie Richardson, grew up in Beatrice, Alabama. Mom spoke highly of her father and his beautiful singing voice.

During those days of deep-rooted poverty, folks could not afford musical instruments; consequently, whoever had a strong voice and had leadership capabilities could be expected to fill the choir master's gratis job, and there was no doubt who would fill that position in that small Alabama community. Interestingly, Leslie was reportedly a whiz at mathematics which is considered a foundation of music.

After completing high school, Leslie moved to Jackson, Mississippi where he met and married my grandmother. They had two girls: my mom – Lilly Ellen – the oldest, and her sister named Jessie Mae.

My grandmother died shortly after Jessie Mae's birth, and my mother was too young to remember anything about her mother. I am sad to say that I never knew anything about her either - not even her name. Shame, shame.

After the funeral, Miss Lilly's grandfather, Isaac Richardson, went back to Jackson, Mississippi and moved the children back to Beatrice, Alabama where their loving grandparents raised the children in the same Christian spirit they had been blessed with in their respective youths.

My Mom was the product of this generous love and Christian spirit.

From Roots and Shoots to Sprigs and Twigs

Mr. Tom Black was the patriarch of our family - reaching back to the 1700's. He and his wife, Rebecca, begat a daughter named Ellen, who married Isaac Richardson. Together, they begat a son named Leslie Richardson who was the father of my mother, Lilly Richardson, who – thank Providence, begat Walter Harold Richardson: ME!

My angelic wife, Helen, and I have been blessed with eight children. From these eight jewels and their spouses have come nine grandchildren (roster follows).

Going back to Mr. Tom, I have learned that he was born in 1772 and lived to the ripe, very ripe age of 104. Mind you, this was in the age without wonder drugs, no cutting-edge surgery and other medical services, no balanced diets. In fact, one was very fortunate to have access to a horse and buggy to get to a doctor during a life-threatening emergency.

From what I gather, his longevity was attributed in long part to a life of moderation (i.e., Lost Horizons), plus a life of Christian values and one of boundless generosity. His religious affiliation was with the Colored Methodist Episcopal (CME), a faith passed from Mr. and Mrs. Black and their progeny to this generation.

Tom Black entered America (from outer islands) through Charleston, South Carolina (date unknown), and eventually settled in Beatrice, Alabama, where he purchased property and raised his family.

Although he was born during the slave era, he was never a slave. A property owner, he demonstrated his Christian generosity when he gave 23 acres of his land for the CME church and the adjoining graveyard.

He was also known far and wide for his powerful singing voice, a rare gene which has fortunately and thankfully been passed on down in clear evidence with each succeeding generation. What a precious, God-given gift to receive. AMEN!

Children	Born	College Attended	Degree Earned
Walter	Jan 21	Arizona State University	BA Communication
Wayne	Dec 5	Florida State University/Troy State	MS Management
Lillie	Mar 21	Arizona State University	MS Drama
Carmen	May 27	Arizona State University/University of West Florida	M/Education Math
Henri	Apr 09	Okaloosa-Walton Junior College	AS Art
Donna	Jun 02	Okaloosa-Walton Junior College	AS Business
William	Sep 25	Florida State University	BS Dietetic
Carl	Jul 21	Florida A&M University/Washington State University	MS Art

Grandchildren
Alicia, Carl J, Zachary, Marcus, Patricio, Carmen, Rickey, Akaysha, Veronica

Memories Are Made of This

I, Walter Harold Richardson, was born at noon on Wednesday, February 12, 1929, the year that the Great Depression exploded. My birthplace: 407 North Davis Street, Pensacola Florida.

It is my desire to share the tapestry of my life's story so that readers might be provoked to look seriously at their own and to likewise try to weave time and events together. It is my intention to note those significant moments of my life, which had the greatest impact upon my thoughts and actions.

In my humble opinion, there are three essential pillars needed to support a life-long journey to success, and they are *Faith, Hope and Love*. And the greatest of these is **LOVE**. In my estimation, the home is the primary source of <u>Love</u>. The church, the nourishment of <u>Faith</u>; and school, <u>Hope</u> for a better, brighter future. The little boy from Jackson Street was fortunate to enjoy all three. ***"How Great Thou Art"***!

I was the third child born of Lilly Ellen Richardson. My birth marked the sixth generation of Mr. Tom Black who was born during slavery but was never a slave. Mr. Tom Black was born in 1772 and died in 1876. He lived to be 104. I am told he lived a devout Christian live.

My grandfather Leslie had a very powerful singing voice, a talent inherited from his grandfather, Mr. Tom. I, through the grace of God, too, have been blessed with a very powerful singing voice that has been passed down from both gentlemen.

I have been told that character can be developed during pregnancy, and Mom said that she adopted a pleasant disposition while she was pregnant with me. I believe my ability to get along with others is the result of Mom's pleasant nature. She later told me that she had experienced numerous unpleasant events, which she preferred not to repeat, during two other pregnancies. She was determined not to let this happen to her again while she was carrying me. She said maintaining that good nature worked.

She recalled when I was born; there was a remarkable difference from the two previous births. When I was born, I appeared to be at peace and very loving and wherever she would lay me down, I would never turn or move, and I remained in place until she came back and picked me up.

Her initial plan was to give me up for adoption. She had made this promise to a family who was unable to have children. Since she was unemployed and already had one child, she did not think she could properly provide for another. My dad would never consider taking this responsibility. He was married and had turned his back on being my real dad. The beginning of my life was like standing in sinking sand, a life with an unwed mother and a dad in denial. ***Over time, I grew to realize that my real father was God, and it was His plan for me to have life and that He would never disown me.*** The spirit of Tom Black was alive and well within me. With this spirit, I would be able to survive during the racial and cultural transition throughout the difficult years ahead. I would advance in age, growing up as a God-fearing man. I could feel the prayers Mr. Tom had offered for over 100 years and for all of us who would follow, bearing his genes. I was born 53 years after his death.

Mom explained why she never regretted changing her mind about giving me up for adoption. Her refusal to go through with the adoption did fracture the friendship with the adoptive family.

I am so very grateful that she changed her mind. She became the best mother one could ever dream of having. Lilly loved us dearly and for 52 years we enjoyed each other. I cannot think of anything anyone else could have given me that would have exceeded the love that Mom provided. One of her sayings that I remember was, ***"Never burn down***

bridges behind you because you never know when you will have to back up."

In essence, she had no problem turning the other cheek. To some, this would have seemed cowardly, but I soon learned that fighting never resolved anything. Scars lingered long after the confrontation was over. Practicing this concept caused me to avoid unnecessary arguing and fighting. I can count only two fights that I was involved in, and I admit that I ran away from quite a few.

It was an honor for me to give the eulogy at Mom's funeral. This was a promise she never thought that I would be able to fulfill. It was hard, but I did it. At the end of the sermon, I sang a song I had composed entitled, *"A Mother's Love."*

Growing up as an only son with two sisters can be fun, but I had to learn early on which one I could tease and which one I couldn't.

I loved to play and go barefoot. I made most of the things I played with, including my own wagon, sling shots, bow and arrows, kites and skateboards. My skateboard was different from the ones seen today. I made mine from skates I had received at Christmas time.

It didn't take much of an effort for Mom to please me. Whatever she bought for me was great and, whenever I came across something that I thought she would like, I would share it with her.

When I was three years old and before we moved from our house on Larue Street, we lived next door to Mrs. Worley who would give me food. I would accept it and take some of it home to Mom. When I needed something from Mrs. Worley, I would go over to the fence around her house and call her. This very kind lady would always answer my call and respond favorable. I was baptized in Allen Chapel AME Church and Mrs. McMillan was my Godmother.

In 1932, Mom gave birth to Dorothy. *After that we moved to 311 East Jackson Street,* where the most incredible years of my life were spent, and where the question was raised – *"What good could come off of Jackson Street in Pensacola, Florida?"*

During my youth, I never considered myself different from other kids in my neighborhood. As expected of kids, we did many of the same things and much of the time got in trouble for doing most of them. Mom always kept a peach tree switch handy to correct the wrongdoings.

I grew up enjoying home and church. Mom taught us our evening prayers, such as, ***"Now I lay me down to sleep, I pray the Lord my soul to keep. If I should die before I wake, I pray the Lord my soul to take."***

Most of the year, the weather was nice, so we slept with the windows opened. At the end of our prayer, we prayed for family members and after those names were called, we would say, ***"God bless everybody."*** One night a man walking by responded, ***"Thank you."***

My affection for church did not disturb me when Mom insisted on us going to Sunday school and remaining for 11 o'clock services. Sunday was a holy day on which we were taught to serve God and rest. We can trace this back to the spirituality of Mr. Tom Black. Admittedly, attending church was not done totally for religious reasons; I went mostly because it was also a social gathering. Without telephones and other means of communications, it was at church that we met most of our friends. I was also there because of obedience to my Mom. Again, it was more like entertainment than spirituality. I really enjoyed the preaching. I waited to see who would be the first to shout. Mom sang in the choir, and she had a good view of us in the pews. So when we started laughing, she would catch our eye and we knew we were in trouble. Yet, it was hard to resist laughing when one of the church members began shouting and others would walk the aisle and proclaim the Lord loudly. I knew what was going to happen when I got home. The peach tree switch would get some action.

I later figured out why those souls would get happy, and the spirit would cause them to cry. The burdens of poor jobs, segregation, and discrimination were terribly hard to bear, so they would cry out to God for mercy. I watched Mom cry many times and I would fight back the tears as I sucked my thumb, because I was old enough to understand the hardships she bore in trying to raise three children alone.

I found humor in one situation with regards to one of our church's members who was very heavy and had a large bust. She really liked a certain gentleman and she seemed to time it perfectly and would get happy every time he walked past her. Maybe it was just my imagination, but it seemed that even if they were taking the collection and this man would pass by this lady, she would start shouting just to get his attention, and he would try to console her. As he tried to restrain her, she would move his arms up around her bosom. Needless to say, I got in trouble because I could never hold back my laughter. Mom would cast a glance in my direction and I would remain still and suck my thumb, knowing what was going to happen when I got home.

This punishment was never abusive. Mom spanked, but it was always for a reason. I cried more after the spanking when Mom would sit near me to explain why she had punished me. She would say, "I spank you because I love you and want you to do what is right." She would continue, saying, "I would die if I had to watch someone else whip you, someone like a policeman." I obeyed and never had to receive any punishment from a policeman or any other person.

To survive in that environment on Jackson Street and in the years ahead, required ***self-determination, the second principle of Kwanzaa, an African observance.*** We both knew that this valuable personal trait had to be worked out and practiced constantly. She knew that to obtain the success I was destined to achieve, I would need to develop it in me.

There were some very frightening incidents that occurred at our home on Jackson Street. Unexpectedly, one night after I had gone to bed, three members of the Ku Klux Klan (KKK) burst into our home. They were hooded, but we knew who they were. They claimed that they were looking for a white child that they were told had entered our house. This was true, but that white child had been left at our house while her parents went out for a social occasion. In modern times it would have been called babysitting. Mrs. Carrie, one of our roomers, knew the white parents and agreed to keep the child while they attended that special activity. I was the only male in the house at the time. Although I was not touched, I was frightened half to death. This kind of forced entry was uncommon, but this first and last time that it happened to us left a deep impression on my psyche. I was never told who had informed those men about the white child being in our house, but I suspected they thought the child had been kidnapped.

Although the term, ***self-determination***, suggests colliding head-on with unexpected situations, it requires perseverance and should be nourished with an abundance of patience in these very hard times in history. Following World War I and on the eve of the Depression, we knew survival required developing self-dependency. We had to fully utilize the resources we had available to us. My Mom's determination would help us through those difficult years.

Being colored and living on Jackson Street was not a glorified situation. Jim Crow laws were the governing factor as to where colored people could drink water or use other public facilities. I was fortunate because our home was a haven of peace. I had disciplined myself to keep clear of any conflicts, which could result in violence. Therefore, I never experienced any physical racially related abuse. The Depression and resulting high unemployment could have easily created stress with us children feeling the brutal effects, but I was, once again, fortunate to live in a Christian home where whatever we had, we shared with each other.

I always felt my home on Jackson Street was blessed because as always, Mom carried the spirit of Tom Black inside her. She knew the Lord, and she worshiped him devoutly. We knew what it was to pray, and we prayed together a lot. Although she had a good education, Mom did domestic work. She had taught school in Beatrice, Alabama prior to the hardship she had experienced which later drove her away from home to live in Pensacola, Florida.

Mom really lived the life of a self-determined individual. Therefore, it was somewhat easy for me to adopt that lifestyle. I learned that loving God would provide the courage and support needed to travel through the days, weeks, months and years ahead of me. I likewise, had to disregard the negative statements like: ***"This boy will never amount to much and is most likely not to succeed."***

The neighborhood surrounding us on Jackson Street had a mixture of alcoholics and gamblers. Common-law marriage was much in evidence. Bootleg whiskey was sold, far too much profanity was overheard and fights developed often, to say the least. It was not the best environment in which to be raised, and if compared to today's environment, it would be considered the ghetto. I was keenly aware that some bad things were going on around us, but I was determined not to allow myself to be overwhelmed by such negative activities. Yes, I grew up there, but with the strong encouragement from my Mom and my own convictions, I was able to remain optimistic about my future. As a dreamer, I felt deeply in my heart that there was more to life than what was taking place on Jackson Street.

In 1934, God was to be glorified in my life. I contracted pneumonia. Mom was unemployed and I was very sick. After using all the old home remedies, she leaned heavily on God, praying that I would be spared. Having lost one child to a tragic fire in Alabama, she did not want to lose her only son. Desperately she prayed, and after a short while, a man appeared and instructed her to take me to Sacred Heart Hospital. Mom resisted because she did not have the money to pay for a doctor or hospital services. The man insisted and Mom finally agreed. Until the day of Mom's death, she could not tell me who that man was, and she never saw him again. I will always believe it was an angel sent by God to answer her prayers. The people at the hospital accepted me and told Mom to go home, that they would take good care of me. Again, I believe the same man who told Mom to take me to the hospital also took care of the arrangements. All this took place when I was too sick to remember anything going on. Mom awaited the news that I had passed away, but the Lord did answer her prayers and after 3 days, I showed signs of recovering. When I first remembered anything, I was in the arms of a nun. She was rocking me when I awakened. After my stay in the hospital, the doctor told Mom to take good care of this boy because he would grow up to be a good man. These were the first positive words that I had ever heard concerning me after so much negative talk earlier. This little boy from Jackson Street had been blessed by God and had been cared for in His Son's Sacred Heart Hospital.

The long-range vision of God was affixed on the years ahead when I would be ordained as a Deacon in the Catholic Church. To me, it fit <u>His</u> plan, and now I am devoting my life in service to His church.

When I returned home from the hospital, it was the very first time I had ever seen my Dad. I. V. Boller was a married man with two children. After my illness, I had to learn how to walk again. I practiced walking between my Mom and my Dad.

Because of my illness, I was late starting school. I attended A. M. DeVaugh Elementary School on Chase Street in Pensacola. I completed two years within one year. The schools were segregated and Mom did not feel that the colored schools were properly provided for. She found private schools in which to enroll her three children. Rebecca went to one, and Dorothy and I went to another. To pay for the tuition for these private schools, Mom took in additional washing and ironing. Again, *self-determination* drives *self-discipline*. We were taught that all of this would be naught without the help of God. ***Mom insisted that we place God before all things***. These were the preparation days for the challenges I would face in the years to come.

Our Sunday school group consisted of young boys. Mr. Nick Williams, our instructor, was a general contractor and a wonderful man . . . he was a great role model. He came to Sunday school well prepared, knew that I studied my lesson and that I was ready to answer the questions he asked. Preparing himself before Christmas, he could tell the Gospel's narrative about the birth of Jesus Christ as though he was in that manger with Mary and Joseph and the infant baby. This was good for me. I needed a deeply spirit-filled man in my life who really loved Jesus and shared that affection with us. At this time, I was enrolled in school with Mrs. Lillie James, who taught school in Pensacola for over 40 years. She started her school to teach her own children because she too had little confidence in the public school system. Mom, who believed deeply in education, heard about her and enrolled Dorothy and me. Mrs. James knew how to teach the basics. We learned reading, writing, and arithmetic. She was a devoted Christian. Now we had the combination of home, church, and school all focused on the love of God and able to explain it as we lived it.

Mom was extremely pleased with the progress that Dorothy and I were making while attending Mrs. Lillie James' school. Mom agreed that education should have some spirituality included. At the beginning of the school day, we would rise when Mrs. James entered the classroom. All the students would sing, "Good morning to you, good morning Mrs. Lillie, good morning to you." We remained standing and recited a short prayer and then the pledge of allegiance to our flag. We were allowed to be seated as we together sang the Roman numerals, followed by the times tables. At the end of this ritual, the students would say in a loud voice, "And 12 times 12 is 144." When the opening ceremony was over, which took place every morning during the school year, Mrs. Lillie called the roll.

With six grades involved, the school day was very long, and Mrs. Lillie would lead them through all their assignments. We arrived at school at eight o'clock in the morning and were dismissed after three in the afternoon. During the autumn and winter months, it would be dark when we walked to school and dark when we finally got home in the evening. Of course, there was always homework to complete.

Our recess was fun, as we used the unpaved road in front of the school for games. After recess, we were instructed to rest. We placed our heads on our desks and, for a few minutes, remained silent. Many of us fell asleep, which was alright with Mrs. Lillie who wanted us to develop this habit of combining recreation with rest while blending education with it all.

BULLETIN: Mrs. Lillie was the mother of the first African-American, United States Air Force, four-star general.

General Daniel "Chappie" James was the youngest son of Mrs. Lillie James!!

It was fun when he had a day out of high school. During our recess, Chappie would challenge all of the smaller boys in a football game. A large child who was very strong whenever he ran the football, he would drag most of us across the goal line with him. I remember once when we were able to trip Chappie and all the kids piled on. We really forced his face into the dirt and held him down while he struggled to free himself from our grip. This was a great thrill to experience! Finally, the bell rang and we had to get back in to the school house.

As we were unpiling one by one, Chappie became very upset, and he really had a bad temper. We were able to run fast enough to get into the school before he caught us. His mother would not allow him inside the school. We had a good laugh watching Chappie standing in the door with dirt all over his face and head.

Along with teaching us the required courses, Mrs. Lillie would teach us about *self-discipline and commitment*. Her theme was, *"Keep your bags packed because you will need to be ready when the door of opportunity opens for colored boys and girls."*

She had vision. She could perceive what would happen in the future for those prepared. I took what she said to heart. I loved Mrs. Lillie as though she was my very own mother. She was a devout Christian and also a member of our church. Allen Chapel, AME Church, was the church for a large number of successful colored people. Chappie and all his family attended. One profound spiritual impression that Mrs. Lillie made upon me was during the holy season of Lent when she would have us observe the sacrifice Jesus had made for us.

On Good Friday she would have us fast during the morning. Just before noon she would have us pull up our chairs around her desk where she would then tell us about the Passion of our Lord and how much he had suffered for our salvation. There was not a dry eye among us. She would dramatize Jesus' suffering. A singer as well, she would sing, "Were You There When They Crucified My Lord?" This deep love that she expressed still lives with me today some 70 years later. After she had finished sharing the Passion with us, one student asked, "Did Jesus do this for colored people, too?" Mrs. James was quick to reply, "Yes, He did it for everyone." We were told to never forget that. "This is how much Jesus loves the Father and us, too."

Easter was a great day for me. I knew that Mom would buy something new for me and Dorothy and Rebecca to wear to church. One Easter, I had decided to stitch a pair of trousers to make drapes out of them. This was the style for almost all of the boys in my grade at school. Whoever could afford them purchased drapes and wore them. I wanted a pair but did not have a job and was not going to ask Mom to buy them for me. This was going to be my Easter Sunday dress trousers. Mom coyly watched me sew the bottom of the trousers, which Mrs. Ruby, a white neighbor, had given to me. I had worked on them for several days and on Holy Saturday, I pressed them and had them ready for Easter Sunday to wear to church. Well, before I could get dressed, Mom came into the room bringing with her a new blue suit, and it really looked good. I never got a chance to wear the drapes that I had sewn together. Dorothy and Rebecca both received new dresses. Easter church services were well attended, and we could always expect a great service.

I earlier mentioned that singing is in my genes. I started singing with the youth choir at Allen Chapel where I first met Helen. Little did I know that one day she and I would be married and spend a wonderful lifetime together.

As I lived in this extraordinary environment, embracing a mother with a deep love for God, and attending Sunday school, having a great role model as a Sunday school teacher, and having a teacher during the week who taught that the love of God was the best combination to override any negative comments expressed by those who did not think that **anything good could come from Jackson Street** . . . I had to agree – "How Great Thou Art!"

Elementary school is a critical period in a child's development and I needed a good foundation to face the years ahead. Upon this foundation I would face the greatest Cultural Revolution or civil rights movement ever occurring any place in the world. I would not only have to be a part of these difficult years, but in some way, make a significant contribution. Facing the comments of ***most likely not to succeed*** had minimum impact on the mind and heart of this little boy from Jackson Street. Mom had accepted the responsibility to train me to love God, my real father, and how to come to know Him personally. Mrs. Lillie James had supported that with God's love for all children, regardless of race, color or creed. She had inspired me to walk proudly and not allow anyone to take away from me the gift from God of being who He created me to be. Mr. William taught me not to be ashamed to claim God in my daily walk of life. We were told to address everyone with respect. Even when we knew the neighborhood drunk, he was still "mister," or when we knew the lady of the night, she was still "miss."

Growing up on Jackson Street had all the temptations to distract me from my path of life. Yet, I was determined to remain on course. I had witnessed some of the hardships Mom had endured and her ***faith*** remained firm. I made a personal pledge that I would never do anything in my life, no matter where I may be or how old I may be, that would offend my mother. I am still living that pledge even though Mom has been dead for many years. She had suffered enough during her long life.

An interesting period in my life was the summer months. During school vacation, Mom would send Rebecca and yours truly to Beatrice, Alabama to help our grandfather harvest the cotton. The train ride was exciting. Our train station in Pensacola was segregated. The white people had one section and the colored had another. The colored people would ride in the front passenger car and the white people had the back cars, just the reverse of the situation when riding on public buses.

The train ride took a full day, so Mom would prepare a lunch for Rebecca and me to take on the train. I would have my portion eaten before we were out of the station in Pensacola. When Grandpapa met us at his end, he would have Isaac, my uncle, with him. Several months younger than I, Isaac would have a straw hat waiting for me to wear to the field. Work started very early in the morning. It was dark when we loaded all the things on the wagon and took off to the crops. I enjoyed the wagon ride as well as picking the cotton. We had quotas to meet and, for a child, it took a lot of work to pick 100 pounds of cotton in one day. I tried, but failed.

Throughout the field were watermelon patches. Isaac and I would pick some at the start of the work day and place them in the cool-water stream running through the field. At noon, when we stopped to eat, we would retrieve the melons which were cool and delicious.

A young female adult, who was mentally retarded, was living in Beatrice at that time. Some would say that she was crazy. I was told that she would chase people and, because she was "out of it"; she would run continuously and never knew when she was tired. I grew up quite scared of many things during my early years and this situation regarding her added to my list.

We were returning from the field one evening and came upon her and her husband near a stream of water. Her husband asked if we would give her a ride across the water. Isaac agreed and when her husband lifted her up onto the wagon, I waited a moment, and then I jumped off. When I looked back, she was trying to pull Isaac's straw hat off while her husband was trying to restrain her. I started running because I was afraid that she would get off the wagon and chase me. I had run more than a mile when a noise came out of the bushes where I was running. My first thought was that she had caught up with me. I ran faster. When I reached the yard, Grandma was there and she saw me running very fast. When I reached the house, she asked why I was running; was something wrong with Isaac? I told her what had happened and how this crazy women got on our wagon and I thought she was chasing me. Grandma started laughing and couldn't stop. She began teasing and saying, "You will see her tonight with her unbraided hair and with half her clothes on, just like she looked today when you left the wagon." I was so afraid, I asked Grandma if I could sleep with her that night, but she said, "No", and I cried.

It was amazing to me when I watched how Grandma and Ernestine, my aunt, could get all the housework done throughout the week and were finished by noon on Saturday. Sunday meal was cooked and everything was cleaned, including scrubbing the front porch and the steps. The yard was raked.

We took our usual Saturday evening bath and all were ready for Sunday worshiping. We attended Sunday school and 11 o'clock service where the collection never exceeded $1. This was the gathering time for the people in the community who would bring their food to church and after the worship services were over, they would bring out the feast. This was good eating. The children played and the afternoon passed quickly. It was dark when we got home on Sunday evening. My Grandpa was a great singer with talent inherited from Tom Black, his grandfather.

Mom would not allow anyone else to spank us. She felt that it was her responsibility to correct us. Well, while we were in Beatrice, Alabama, Isaac and Rebecca decided to go for a walk. To walk around the block in Beatrice was quite different from walking around the block on Jackson Street. So, we took off without permission, and walked a long way before we reached a turning point. It turned out, we had walked to town; we were actually in Beatrice. We started the long walk back home, but when we arrived, we learned that Grandma had left home looking for us. When she returned, she told our grandfather we needed a spanking for running off. Isaac and I began to cry before Grandpa could gather the switches. I questioned Isaac about whether or not Grandpa would use the razor sharpening strap hanging on the wall? Isaac said, "No," and I asked what he would use? He said a switch from one of the trees in the yard. We both continued to cry. Grandpa never rushed when doing anything so by the time he finally got back and started spanking us, it had taken over an hour. Rebecca got off easy, she pulled her dress down below her feet and Grandpa could only get to a small portion of her body. Not so with Isaac and me. He just held us up and spanked us. I think we cried more before the spanking than afterwards. We never went walking again.

Isaac and I would make our own wagon. We took boards and made a box, sawed down a small pine tree and cut wheels from the trunk. We had a small swimming hole in the pasture where we would go swimming. It had been so much fun when the summer was running out and the time for us to return home was approaching.

When we returned home, we spent a lot of time explaining to Jean and Eloise what a fun time we had had. We really wanted Jean and Eloise to go to Beatrice with us. Dorothy would go when she was older. She would spend time with Bertha, our Aunt Oshea's daughter, who was being raised by Grandma. Oshea had moved to Pensacola and was living with Mom. Bertha became my favorite cousin. We really loved each other.

I considered my visits to Beatrice as a period in my life when I was free to do some of the things I was afraid to do in Pensacola. These things were not bad but it seemed as though I was free. I did not have to contend with the daily problems caused by discrimination. There, the community was all black people and we only had contact with white people when we went to town.

I got my first job when I was 12 years old, shining shoes at Mr. Bateman's barber shop. Whatever I earned, I would take home and give to Mom, who kept the money for me even though I really wanted her to use it. She saved it, however, and at Christmas, 1941, I was surprised with a brand new bicycle.

With the new "wheels," I was able to get a job working at the store next door to us. The store was owned by the Malamos, a kind Greek family who did not show any signs of prejudices. For them, I proudly delivered groceries over most of the eastern section of town.

During my teenage years, I worked part time at Mustin Beach Officer's Club. I started as dishwasher. Other "positions" included pots and pans, supply clerk, short order

cook, bus boy, and finally, a waiter.

I was allowed to work on Sundays after attending church services, during which time I earned enough money to purchase my first watch, a Bulova, which I left unattended in the locker room, and someone stole it.

Mr. Sam Taylor taught me how to wait on tables and became a very close friend.

I had completed my 6th grade at Spencer Bibbs Elementary School. Mrs. James had laid the foundation for me to re-enter public school with the necessary discipline to excel. This I did.

It was at Spencer Bibbs School that I had my first fist fight. Billy insisted on pushing me around, and I finally struck back. Although there was no winner, we later became good friends. During the school year I had a chance to witness my faith and share my position with regards to girls. I was vocal about avoiding sexual intercourse. Mr. Williams had taught us during Sunday school that this was not the right thing to do. So, I would tell the other boys the same. They began calling me "revelation." I developed a great respect for females very early in my life. This again goes back to my love for Mom and my commitment to never do anything, regardless of where I was, that would reflect unfavorably on her. Throughout the rest of my school years, this nickname stuck with me, and even today, those who grew up with me call me "Rev."

After completing my elementary education in 1942, I entered Booker T. Washington High School.

Containing the necessary ingredients to develop a life worthy of God's blessing, my early life, I would have to say, was quite fruitful.

Jackson Street can be found in many cities throughout the country, but the situation that I grew up in does not differ much from those in many other communities around the world. Greatness does not always come from upper class families or from expensive dwellings. The future was ahead of us. The little boy from Jackson Street had discovered his purpose for life through the guidance of his Mom at home (*The Pillar of Love*) and the teaching of Mrs. Lillie James at school *(The Pillar of Hope)* and Mr. Williams at church *(The Pillar of Faith)*. These people are credited with making an everlasting impression on my life that would support and propel me through the years ahead. The Greek who owned the grocery store next door and gave Mom the leftover bread and the vegetables that were too withered to be sold – was enlightening – and opened my eyes and heart to be generous and to share whatever I have with others. The white families in the neighborhood, who gave Mom the clothes that their children had outgrown, were an inspiration. When I gathered all these good deeds together, they fulfilled the gospel that Jesus spoke about: "When I was hungry, you fed me and when I was naked, you clothed me."

There was a wide range of religious beliefs and practices. Some were Baptists, others were Holiness, and there were Catholics. This mixture of religions reflected God's diversity and that everyone has the right to His graces and blessings.

Blessings included my love for my sister, Rebecca, the oldest, and Dorothy, the youngest of the three. We grew up with tremendous respect for each other. Rebecca was not as friendly as Dorothy, but this went back to the situation Mom shared about the difficulties she experienced while pregnant with her first child. Rebecca has a beautiful singing voice. She was likewise, a good student but she differed with Mom at times and this did not always end up very favorably. Dorothy was different because she, too, was born with the pleasant disposition which Mom developed and said that she would maintain whenever she would carry another child. Dorothy and I would share our toys and other pleasures with each other, but Rebecca would not always participate. Although she would not always get involved with what we were doing, everyone still loved her and there were times when she shared her love with us, too. Mom did everything possible to please her but, too often, her efforts fell short of the mark. Although I never wanted to do anything that would upset Mom, there were times when I had very unfortunate experiences that grieved me tremendously.

One time, it was soon to be Mother's Day. I had earned enough money to purchase a gift for Mom: a small box of embroidered handkerchiefs. I had them wrapped and put the gift away until the big event. On that early morning when I got up to give her the gift, I could not find it. I cried harder than I ever recall crying at any time before or since. Mom tried to console me but nothing worked. I really wanted her to have that gift and, thank God, she knew it. Throughout the years, whatever I gave her seemed to fall short of that one precious gift that I wanted so much for her to have.

These were the early years of my life. How little did I know that the years ahead would be full of God's blessings. Would the question, "What good would come from Jackson Street in Pensacola, Florida?" ever be answered? Read on.

George Booker, my best friend, and I played together and competed against one another when making kites. His dad was a baker and frequently invited us to come and enjoy hot donuts. Willie Allen was also a good friend but not always willing to play the games that George and I played.

Jean and Eloise were our next-door neighbors. We claimed each other as brothers and sisters and still do today.

Mr. Henry James, who rented a room from Mom, was considered a big brother to me. He pressed clothes at a laundry. Mrs. Carrie looked after us when Mom was away. Most of our ball games were played on the unpaved street in front of our house. Billie, a white kid who lived around the corner from our house, would come over and play with us.

He enjoyed Mom's cooking. The newspaper boy would not go down through the alley connecting Jackson Street with Larue, so he paid me a nickel a week to deliver his papers.

I really enjoyed my youth. I am convinced that it was the spiritual threads *(Faith, Hope & Love)* that kept it all knitted together.

Our favorite movie star was Shirley Temple and favorite cowboy was Gene Autry. The movies were segregated with a separate colored entrance which didn't seem to deter us from going to see Shirley Temple.

As I look back over my early years, I realize that a life connected to God, our real father, is full of real joy. I learned that most setbacks are temporary and the real danger is allowing unfortunate situations to control the mind. The mind should be driven by the love in your heart. The cement that holds the three pillars together is spirituality. This common thread of spirituality has the strength to endure the torments of time. Even in my youth, I was able to shed the things that were unpleasant: kinda' like Oprah Winfrey in "The Color Purple." The comments of *"most likely not to succeed and not amounting to much,"* became rungs on the ladder of success which I had imagined I would someday climb.

Mr. Henry Taylor was the one who first observed my spirituality. When the kids would get together to have church services in our backyard; Rebecca, Dorothy, Jean and Eloise (called Red Top) were the choir, I was Reverend Johnson. The choir would start the service with "This little light of mine, I'm going to let it shine." We would follow the outline of the church services used at Allen Chapel with which we were familiar. When the time came for the sermon, I was the preacher. Mr. Henry Taylor listened to one of my sermons and afterward said that someday I was going to be a preacher. The sermons that I preached in our backyard impressed him deeply and thereafter he called me preacher. He was not a frequent church goer.

During the months after World War II had been declared, many food items were rationed. Once in a while on Sunday afternoon, Mom would bake a cake and the community would pool its resources and we would churn some homemade ice cream. Over the years, I have yet to taste ice cream as sumptuous as that creation.

In summary: during these early years, under the circumstances and the environment on Jackson Street, some of the folks I admired and who made a positive impact upon my life were:

Mr. Nick Williams, my Sunday school teacher *(Faith)*;

Mrs. Lillie James, my elementary school teacher *(Hope)*;

Mom, Rebecca and Dorothy *(Love)*;

Mr. Henry James who rented from Mom;

Mrs. Carrie Johnson who rented from Mom and who would watch us while Mom worked;

Mrs. Worley, who gave me food over the fence;

Mrs. McMillan, my Godmother;

Reverend Johnson, Pastor of Allen Chapel, AME Church

Mr. Alfred DeVoux, my stepfather;

Mr. McDaniel, principal of Booker T. Washington High School;

Mrs. Lillie Frazier, my home section teacher during my senior year in high school who gave me a role in the senior class play;

Mr. Nick Malamo, the Greek who owned the grocery store near us;

Mrs. Ruby, the white lady who paid me to chop firewood;

Mrs. Barge, the children's class leader at Allen Chapel; and

Mr. Sam Taylor who taught me how to wait on tables at Mustin Beach Officer's Club.

Others included my Aunt Oshea, who came from Beatrice to live with us. Mom worked hard to arrange things to accommodate her. She became my favorite aunt.

Growing Up

Yes, God is Real

I suppose it is politically incorrect to ask the question: What good could come out of Pensacola, Florida? Well, how about Chappie James, the first African American four-star general in the Air Force; Emmitt Smith, the running back for the Dallas Cowboys; Roy Jones and Walter Richardson.

It all started in February 1929 and the journey has not ended. Growing up as a sickly kid, surviving pneumonia at age four, competing for space between two sisters . . . that's a hard way to start life. Yes, I agree: *it can make you or break you.* Rebecca and Dorothy were great sisters. They both loved me, and I returned the affection. Over time I would make myself available to help them. They could count on me.

As long as I can remember, I was taught that God is real. I learned it at home, at Sunday school and while attending Mrs. Lillie James' elementary school. At church and school we sang, *"Jesus loves me this I know."* When taught during my entire youth that Jesus loved me, I had every reason to believe it was true. I had peers who teased me because of my love for God. Most of the ones who criticized my affection for God had a dad in their homes. I had as my Dad, God. *He is real and he is love.*

Growing up in the neighborhood, I had friends like George, Willie Allen, Eloise, Jean and Marilyn. We grew up really enjoying each other.

They, too, considered it a treat to go to the movies together. The segregated theaters didn't bother them either as we enjoyed Shirley Temple, Roy Rogers, Superman and the tear jerker, *"Nobody Children."*

The doctor who treated me when I was sick at Sacred Heart Hospital told Mom to take good care of me because he could tell from my behavior I would grow up and become a good man. His vision viewed me in the future as doing good things for others, rendering unselfish service, and love wherever life would lead me. Why not?

In 1942, Rebecca – a very good student – graduated from high school but did not want to go to college. She chose to work. The war had begun, and she worked at the Naval Air Station in Pensacola. She met Bruce, who was in the Navy, at the station, fell in love and became pregnant; their planned marriage never happened.

On February 13, 1946 she gave birth to a daughter, Gloria Jean, who was born in the back room on Jackson Street. Mrs. Jones, the midwife who had delivered me, came to deliver Gloria. During the delivery, the back room was restricted from Dorothy and me. We were able to see the baby shortly after it was born and cleaned. This was my first look at a newly born baby, but was not to be the last. *My God is real.*

My high school years were enjoyable. I studied hard, worked after school to help financially, and sang in the choir at our church. Allen Chapel AME Church was where a large number of educated colored people worshiped. Mom's 15-year membership was a continuation and a branch off of her family lineage with CME.

A popular old adage maintains that *nothing remains the same.* The year 1947 arrived. In May, I graduated from high school. It was an emotional moment for Mom and me. The joy caused us to remain wrapped in each other's arms crying. I had achieved the challenge of overcoming the negative comment: *"that boy won't amount to nothing; he is most likely not to succeed."* Thanks Dad . . . **I knew my God was real for I could feel him in my heart. The real joy would remain always with the Depression Baby, the boy from Jackson Street.**

Entry into College . . . and the Military

I believe that whatever happens as life advances, the outcome can usually be attributed to how one reacts to unexpected crises and difficult situations. I believe discipline is a necessary self-imposed behavior. When used during crises, it requires a firm understanding of how God has a plan for each human being. To remain calm in the midst of stress is not easy, but somehow the Christian foundation upon which my early years was built, made it easier than if I had never been taught about God, my real father. Having a solid foundation of Christian discipline came into play and stayed with me throughout the rest of my life.

Upon graduating from Booker T. Washington High School with the class of 1947, I was in the upper 10% of my class. My grades made me eligible to select the college I wished to attend. After Mom wrote to several Negro colleges, a few letters of interest came back, and I selected Alabama State Teacher's College in Montgomery, Alabama, because I thought the science program would better prepare me for medical school, my primary interest. Besides, I was offered a work scholarship at that institution.

It was a joyful yet sad Sunday afternoon in September 1947, when I departed Pensacola to travel to Montgomery. Mom had packed a large lunch for me to have something to eat during the long train ride. It was a sad moment for me because I had never been apart from Mom except for the two weeks we would spend in Beatrice, Alabama visiting my grandparents during the summers. This was different because I began a series of numerous trips in and out of Pensacola to visit Mom.

The train ride to Montgomery went well, but the sadness did not end when I finally arrived at the dormitory. Surprisingly, I found other fellows who were experiencing the same loneliness. As I remember it, there was a lot of crying that night. To top it off, we had to go through an initiation with the upper class men treating us very cruelly. We were pushed about and spanked. This added to more loneliness on my part. That first night on that college campus is something I will never forget.

On the other hand, living away from home for the first time allowed freedom that I was not accustomed to while living at home. There was no one to tell me when I should be home at night, nor was there anyone to tell me it was time to get my lessons done. Thankfully, there was enough self-discipline remaining within me to help me manage my time favorably. I joined a church in Montgomery and was faithful just as if I had been at home.

The Class "C" Scholarship that I chose was as a cook in the campus dining hall. The working hours were from 4 a.m. until 8 a.m. After work, I cleaned up and attended my morning classes, which began at 10 a.m. After regulating my work schedule with my classes, I found time to audition for the famous Alabama State Teacher College Chorus. Thanks be to God, my gift of a good singing voice paid off. I was selected to sing as a baritone.

Financially, my scholarship aided tremendously in covering the cost of my classes. It did not provide extra spending money, but Mom would send me $5.00 each month, and the money she sent always came in mighty handy. However, to make it financially, I applied for a part-time waiter's job in downtown Montgomery at the Whitney Hotel.

Although I worked as a cook in the dining hall, it did not mean that I was allowed to eat as much as I wanted to. On nights when I was called to work at the Whitney Hotel, I would gather the leftovers and bring them back to the dormitory to share with the students living near my room. Word got around when I was called to work because they knew that I would bring home some kitchen treasures. Whenever I returned, those who had waited up for me greeted me as a hero. They knew that I would share what I had brought home. Other students who worked for the same hotel would go directly to their rooms and lock the doors. Sharing was definitely not a high priority. Consequently, what Mom had taught me all through my life about sharing with others carried over at college and continued throughout the years.

My work in the dining hall, as well as my grades, were going very well. Mail from home was always encouraging and inspiring. It was a comfort when Mom kept me abreast of what Dorothy and Rebecca were doing.

A few months into the first term, enrollment increased and living adjustments had to be made. A few students living in Dillar's Hall were asked to move to the lower section of the gymnasium. I volunteered because a very nice and roomy section had been selected to be used as a dorm. I was only there a few days when I undressed to take a shower and for the first time that I could remember, I took off my high school class ring and placed it on the outside of my locker. I wasn't gone long, but when I returned, the ring was gone. I cried so hard because it had taken all the money that Mom and Rebecca could scrape up for me to buy that ring during my senior year. I was bitterly sad because that ring meant so much to me.

Before returning home for the Christmas holidays, my God-given singing voice allowed me to sing, for the first time, Handel's Messiah, with the Alabama State Choir. The group was well known, the auditorium was jam-packed, and it was considered a great performance. The little boy from Jackson Street was singing with this great choir and this was assuredly a high point of his young life.

In January 1948, I returned to college, kept studying hard, while still working at the dining hall on campus and at the Whitney Hotel. In April 1948, of my freshman year, the students finally got disgusted with the food in the dining hall on campus and organized a boycott. On that day, I overslept after working late the night before at the downtown hotel. When I arrived an hour late, Mrs. Johnson fired me, accusing me of participating in the boycott. Even after telling her the truth about oversleeping, she stood firm on discharging me. Well, I knew this would place a heavy burden on Mom to pay the full tuition for the final two months of school.

Soon, the situation on campus reached the Governor's office and he called Dr. Trenholm, President of the college, to ask what was going on. Dr. Trenholm said that the students were unhappy with the food and the Governor retorted, "Feed them." For the first time in that entire year, we were fed pork chops, mashed potatoes and rolls. This was a long way from the Spam and creamed corn that we had been fed daily. One student got carried away and posted a pork chop bone on the student bulletin board in the administrative building.

After I lost my job in the dining room, I asked for more hours of work at the hotel to help cover my tuition. Studying hard, I finished my freshman year with a 3.2 grade point average.

I returned home to a very proud Mom who was working at the Naval Air Station, and she invited me to come meet her coworkers. She was elated as she escorted me through the offices and introduced me to the naval officers and high ranking civilians. Mom, you see, was a "custodian." In other words, she kept the restrooms clean.

Mom and my step dad, Alfred Devoux, had made great progress with improving our new home on North Haynes Street, but she still needed permanent windows.

Dorothy was entering her senior year in high school. Rebecca had one child (Gloria Jean) and had moved to Cleveland, Ohio, while Mom kept Gloria.

Soon, I was fortunate to get a job offer waiting tables at the Magnolia Club in Fort Walton Beach, Florida. When I accepted, I had never traveled east of Pensacola or as far as Fort Walton Beach. The Bishop brothers were the owners of the Magnolia Club and Mr. Leon Bishop learned that I was a college student who was working during the summer to earn money for my sophomore year. Generously, he gave me extra work to increase my take-home pay. At the end of the summer, I had earned enough to cover my entire year of tuition. I paid for the new windows for Mom's home and purchased clothes to take back to college.

I was dating Johnnie Mae whenever I was home from college or from work in Fort Walton Beach. Before leaving for college, Mr. Leon Bishop promised to help me financially if the need arose. I was a good dancer, and I could dance while balancing a large aluminum tray. One night while the club band was playing an upbeat number, I came out of the kitchen spinning the tray and dancing. The crowd got excited and began throwing money out on the dance floor. I kept dancing, not knowing whether or not I would be fired when I finished. After the music was over, I swept up nearly $20.00. Mr. Leon called me over and asked where I had learned to dance like that. I told him I learned that routine while working at the Officer's Club at the Naval Air Station in Pensacola. He said, "When we have a band again, I want you to come out and dance for them." I eventually danced enough to make more money on a Saturday night than any of the other waiters.

Fort Walton Beach was a gambling city. I would compare it with the Biloxi, Mississippi of today. Gambling was wide open.

The only black club in Fort Walton Beach was Nick's, frequented by black men and women who came to Fort Walton to work. I met Mary Burnette during the summer months while working in Fort Walton Beach. Mary's dad owned a café where I would spend time with her after getting off of work. She was a student at Florida A&M College.

The summer passed and I returned to college. Since I did not have to work on campus, I joined the football team. This was exciting to me. Mom would not allow me to play football when I was in high school. Anyway, I made the team. The top thrill of my whole stay at Alabama State was to play football against Tuskegee Institute. During the 1948 Thanksgiving Classic – the game between Alabama State and Tuskegee – I was able to go in for one play. I also played against Morehouse College when Dr. Martin Luther King, Jr. was a student there.

I made a lot of friends at Alabama State. Years later when the Civil Rights Movement began in Montgomery, I remembered how I, too, had ridden the same buses that Rosa Parks rode. I, too, experienced standing when the colored section was full and the white seats were not. The bus that ran down South Jackson Street to the college campus was filled mostly with students; many times it was only black students riding and no whites, so we could use the front seats.

When I returned home from Christmas, 1948, Dorothy approached me and asked if I would consider joining the army and help support her through college. I really loved Dorothy and if this would help her, then I would consider it.

During the Christmas break, I worked for Mr. Bishop at the Magnolia Club. He asked me to help for the New Year's party. I did and when it was time to return to college, once again, Mr. Leon offered to help me if I needed it.

Mom was enjoying what she was seeing in me. She re-emphasized she wanted me to grow up and become a good man, thereby repeating what the doctor had told her after my serious pneumonia illness and recovery at Sacred Heart Hospital. I was really working hard to fulfill her desires. I visited my dad while I was home for Christmas. He was married again, this time to a school teacher, Mrs. Mardese, who was a very good lady. She was kind to me and proud of the manner in which I was handling my teenage years, and she was very vocal about letting me know her positive feelings. My dad was also showing signs of appreciation for the fact that I was using my life to accomplish something. His only natural son was a cook on the railroad diner car for the Sunset Limited Passenger Train. He was married and had two boys. I. V., Jr., who had a serious drinking problem, would eventually die as a result of alcohol. I observed the change in my dad's attitude, which was far different from the early years of denial and reflecting the thinking of those who never thought ***anything good could come from Jackson Street***.

Returning to college after Christmas in January, 1949, I was only back for a week when I heard three guys talking about enlisting in the army. These men would surely have been drafted because their grades would not allow them draft deferment.

I asked if they were really serious about joining the military and if they were planning to join the army, if I could go along with them. We went to the recruiting center in downtown Montgomery and took the tests. After they were graded, the recruiter called out wanting to know, "Who is Walter Richardson?" I raised my hand and he asked to speak with me. After entering his office, he said that I had scored high enough to enter the Air Force if I was interested. I was not sure that I really wanted to do this, but Dorothy had asked me to help her and this was the time of decision. It was Monday, and he told me to let him know before Friday.

On Friday, 13 January, 1949, I enlisted in the United States Air Force. All of this was unknown to Mom. The Air Force was only two years old and segregation persisted. After being sworn into the service, I traveled to San Antonio, Texas, to begin basic training in the last all-colored flight to go through Lackland Air Force Base. President Truman had signed a bill ending segregation in the military. When I arrived at Lackland Air Force Base early Saturday morning, January 14, a truck was at the train station to meet us. We were transported directly to the dining hall on base to have something to eat. After I was sworn in, the recruiting office had given me meal cards to use on the train from Montgomery to San Antonio. The diner did accept the meal tickets but colored travelers had to wait until the white passengers were served first.

Once inside the dining hall at Lackland, much to my surprise, we were offered anything we wanted to eat. I had baked chicken, bread and milk. After we finished eating, we were escorted to our barracks. It was near three o'clock in the morning when I finally got in bed, but I had a full stomach and had settled in bed to sleep until about noon after a long trip.

It seemed as though I had just laid down when the Drill Sergeant entered the barracks and yelled, "Get out of those beds." I stayed still because I was sure it was not meant for me since I had just arrived. He came to my bed and asked, "What's wrong with you? You got polio? Get out of that bed." I got up and put on that nice grey suit and those grey suede shoes I had traveled there wearing. Still half asleep, we were marched to the same dining hall I had left just an hour ago. It didn't seem like the same place. The eggs were green and the potatoes were burnt and the KPs were rude. I began to think I had made a terrible mistake leaving college and entering the military without talking this over with Mom. Here I was, loaded down with self-pity, which was overriding the usual strong self-determination that I had attempted to develop over the years. I forced myself to eat some of the food that was on my tray. It wasn't long before the Drill Sergeant yelled, "Attention" and ordered us out of the dining hall to the road. He instructed us on how to get in formation, starting with the tallest and down to the shortest, and I fit somewhere in the middle. After we marched to the indoctrination center, we were told to remove our civilian clothes and to place them in the box provided and after, to take a shower and get into the military underwear and fatigues. We received a haircut and followed a green line until we finally reached the medical station where the medics were waiting with several shots. I had never before been "shot" that many times, so much so that they had to use both arms. We received a full complement of clothing except for shoes. The newly formed United States Air Force had run out of shoes. It was fine with me because I had worn those grey suede shoes, but not so for many others. Some had come with tennis shoes. Remember, this was January in San Antonio, Texas. It was very cold.

By noon, we had completed the tour through the indoctrination center and went back to the mess hall. Incidentally, "mess" was a much better description of this facility than dining hall. The same KP's were on duty and was as rude as before. I took what they served and went to my seat with the others. By this time, the shots were beginning to grow very painful. My arms hurt so much; I couldn't raise them to scratch my head. I cried. We were permitted to "hit the sack" early that Saturday evening because we were all so full of pain.

On Sunday morning, we marched to church services, but I didn't mind. The service was good. I sang because I knew most of the songs. We were allowed to rest after Sunday church service. I figured this was as good a time as any to write home and let Mom know what was going on, so I did. I had enough money to buy a stamp. I mailed Mom the letter and explained why I had left college. I was told that when she received the letter, she fainted at the mailbox. She was completely unaware that I had left college and had entered the military. It was really hard for her to accept. In her eyes, her little Walter had made a major decision without checking with her! Little Walter was on the precipice of MANHOOD!! Once I was able to determine how much I was to receive in monthly pay, I arranged it so that $50 of my $75 would go to Mom to help with Dorothy's college tuition.

In May 1949, Dorothy graduated from Booker T. Washington High School with exceptionally good grades and was accepted at Fisk University in Tennessee. The military days ahead would be very challenging. One thing I remember is what S. D. Landrum, a World War II veteran attending Alabama State College, had told me when he learned that I had enlisted in the military, "Walter, you won't like the Army but do what you are told to do and you will make it." This positive advice would support my self-determination as I began my military journey. Although it had never been my intention to enter the military, I knew that I would make the best of it with the help of my Father, God.

After two weeks of drilling in those grey suede shoes, my feet were hurting. I couldn't allow the bed sheet to touch my toes, they hurt so badly. When the supply unit finally received shoes, I ordered a pair two sizes larger to make room for the sore spots. One Saturday when we were enjoying a break, I took those grey suede shoes, soaked them down in cigarette lighter fluid, and set them afire. I wanted to hurt them as badly as they had hurt me. My growing determination was to make the best of this voluntarily-inflicted Air Force life. Always a fast learner, I would use my talents to learn all that I could, regardless of the situation. The weeks began to move faster and I was starting to enjoy it.

One of the outstanding drill instructors was Sergeant English, who was assigned to our flight. After he taught us a few unique drill skills, we grew to enjoy drilling so much that on Saturday evening, when we could have had time off, we used the time to drill and try out the moves that Sergeant English had taught us. At eight weeks (midterm), our flight came in second in drill competition, and at the final 16-week competition, we won the whole caboodle.

At times, the past will swarm back over you. That's what happened to me during basic training. In my junior and senior years in high school, I had to take a foreign language. Spanish was offered but I did not take the course seriously. I never really did learn how to speak the language. At Lackland, the service club would bring young Spanish speaking girls on base to socialize with the troops. I felt so embarrassed because when I was approached by one of these lovely young ladies, I could not communicate with her.

Mid way through our training, we had to make a decision as to what career field we wanted to enter. At that time, all they had to offer colored airmen was cook school or a truck driver's course. I selected truck driver's course because I was 19 years old and had never driven a motor vehicle. Following my selection, a show came to Lackland Air Force Base. It was an all-colored airmen show originating out of Lockbourne Air Force Base, Columbus, Ohio, and the show's name was "Operation Happiness." Lieutenant Daniel "Chappie" James was the Master of Ceremonies, Commander of the show and a pilot. The show was great. After the performance was over, Chappie announced that if anyone was interested in becoming a part of the show there would be auditions the following day. So, I got permission from my First Sergeant to go to the audition and again, my God-given singing voice paid off. After my rendition, I was accepted to join the group and to sing with the singing sergeants which had originated at Lockbourne. Glory be! I never got to go to truck driving school.

After the 16 weeks of basic training was over, I was promoted to private first class and had gained respect and friendship with all of the upper sergeants. Proudly, I had become involved in the Sunday church services.

Now that the training was over, we were assigned to different locations. I was sent to Lockbourne Air Force Base to join up with the show, "Operation Happiness," and to become a member of the world famous Tuskegee Airmen. Colonel B. O. Davis, our commander, would later become the first black general in the U.S. Air Force.

I performed in one show with the group but word came down that the base would be closed to integrate. I received orders to Okinawa, Japan, and Chappie was assigned to the Philippines.

On my visit home, Mom was so proud of me. I had one stripe and the uniform was tailored to fit. Of course, she had to invite me again to the Naval Air Station to show me off to the people working on the floor where she was still the "custodian." The situation clearly illustrated what was said at the beginning of this period in my life in the military: "Whatever happens as life advances, the outcome can be attributed to how one reacts to unexpected crises and difficult situations. To exercise discipline is a necessary self-imposed behavior, when used during a crisis that requires a firm understanding of God and what His plan is for every human being." Unbeknownst to me, God had a very definite plan for me and how my behavior would become a vital part of the growth of this new department of defense, ***The United States Air Force.***

Over the next 30 years, this little boy from Jackson Street would make unprecedented contributions that would, over the years, be remembered.

People who made a good impression that helped me:
– William Stanford, my roommate in college
– Dr. Hardy, Bio-Social teacher
– Dr. King, the choir director
– Kitchen manager of Whitney Hotel
– Sergeant Kitchen, my drill master

The next months following basic training would help tremendously while I sought to adapt to my new military life.

Opportunity Knocks

The time had arrived; another door of opportunity which Mrs. Lillie James, my elementary teacher had spoken of, had opened. Basic Training was over. I had completed 16 weeks of training at Lackland Air Force Base and was assigned to the last all-black flight, ending segregated basic training in the Air Force. I later learned that the Air Force was the first branch of the Department of Defense to end discrimination.

Consequently, I was at the birth of integration in the armed forces and I pondered over the things I had learned at home, church and school and how difficult it would be to associate with white people. I mentally agonized: "Am I ready? Am I really strong enough *spiritually or mentally* to withstand the cruel, brutal beast of *prejudice and discrimination* that stood ahead?" I had seen Mom live through very difficult times and many of the hardships she had endured had been imposed by both Negroes as well as white people.

I remembered Mr. Watson, the white rent man when Mom was short one dollar on the day that the monthly rent of $11 was due. Mom and our renters were ordered out of our house on Jackson Street by noon! Negro neighbors, who could have helped, refused to do so. We moved all of our belongings out on the street. Mr. Henry James, who rented the back room, arrived just before noon with the dollar he had borrowed from a friend. Mr. Watson removed the "for rent sign" he had posted and sternly warned Mom not to let it happen again. It never did.

Somberly, I had observed so many similar unpleasant things happen to our family, but now I was 19 years old and must step out alone in a world full of resentment, hate, evil, uncertainty, racial bias and without the protective blanket of life-long supporters. I had to rely upon the very first principles of my spiritual life: *"God, my true Father; and prayer."*

Throughout my youth, I had been told by Mom that God was my real Father and that He answers *prayer*. I had witnessed trust in Him. He answered prayers and would help overcome the most difficult obstacles placed in life by Satan and his helpers. Now that the time had arrived, I made my decision to remain on a course that had been proved successful for other black achievers. The path ahead was invisible, yet I knew from listening to Mr. Nick Williams, my Sunday school teacher, that God would never abandon you. He said your obedience to God would help you to be obedient to your superiors. That encouragement propped open my mind to remember to do whatever I was told to be worthy of God's blessings. By mentally making this pledge of obedience and trusting in God, I would do what I was told to do and help to affect necessary changes to make the United States Air Force the air superiority power it later turned out to be. My youthful past had been challenging, and the future was uncertain. I had to step out of the dark shadow of racial differences to become instrumental in a changing world. I had to overcome those years of my youth with the haunting sounds of *most likely not to succeed* and make a difference along with significant progress. While enduring the past, **NEVER** did I expect what lay ahead. The door of opportunity was wide open. I chose to enter it and, in the years ahead, I proved without a doubt I had something to offer, and I did.

My first assignment after basic training was the 332nd Fighter Group with the Tuskegee Airmen at Lockbourne Air Force Base, Columbus, Ohio. My trip to Columbus, Ohio was my first entry into a northern state. I found it hard to realize that some buildings were taller than the 10-story First National Bank in downtown Pensacola.

While assigned to Lockbourne, I worked for Master Sergeant James, first sergeant of the Base Support Squadron. Master Sergeant James was an outstanding person who had served in Europe during World War II with the Tuskegee Airmen. He was nearing retirement but was an excellent example and role model for me to follow in executing my military duties. When I arrived at Lockbourne to become a member of Operation Happiness, the show had not returned from touring military bases in California.

Master Sergeant James authorized me to take a few days leave since the show was weeks away from returning. He told me about nearby Wright-Patterson AFB in Dayton, Ohio, where I might get a flight to a base close to my home.

My very first flight was aboard a B-25 aircraft which went to Barksdale Air Force Base, Louisiana. First, I had to be taught how to put on a parachute. Afterward, I entered the aircraft and was invited to sit behind the pilot. I can't remember ever having any fear of flying. When I arrived at Barksdale, I was directed to the transit barrack to rest until the next morning when I would travel by bus to Pensacola. My linen had been issued and I was preparing my bed when a white sergeant came and asked what I was doing? I explained that I was making my bed. He said I couldn't stay there. I asked why. He said I would have to go down to the colored squadron. There was another colored airman with me who had suffered a broken leg. The two of us were escorted to the colored squadron. While we were waiting outside for transportation, another white sergeant came and talked with us. He said he was so disappointed with the way we had been treated and allowed that he had come to realize, since he was stationed there at Barksdale, that the south was still fighting the Civil War. He again apologized for the way we had been treated and I knew precisely what he was saying, but I knew one day we would win this war without weapons. Prayer is more powerful than any weapon mankind will attempt to develop.

That night, we sat up because there was no place to sleep except on the floor. The colored sergeant who came to get us pointed out that two straight-back chairs was all he had to offer. All night we fought mosquitoes. The next day I left by bus to Pensacola and thankfully slept most of the way.

After my one-week leave, I returned to Lockbourne. The white citizens of Columbus impressed me beyond words with their friendly attitudes toward the all-colored military unit stationed there. For the first time, I rode in the front of a public bus and no one asked me to move back. Police officers would place drunken airmen on a bus back to the base rather than confine them. Colonel B. O. Davis, Jr.

had established outstanding public relations with the local citizens All that I ever heard about him and his command was extremely positive. Consequently, I enjoyed Columbus and joined the choir at one of the local churches.

The show finally arrived back at Lockbourne after a month's tour in California, and I performed with the group before it was disbanded.

In August 1949, Colonel Benjamin O. Davis announced at Commander's call that the Wing was closing. He read an Executive Order signed by President Truman that the Wing was ordered closed to facilitate integration. At that time, in 1949, Lockbourne was the only all-black Wing in the Air Force. The following insert taken from Air Force history will help explain how it was God's will that I would remain in the United States Air Force because when the executive order was issued, I did not have an assigned skill. The message read:

"The Air Force Commanders' Conference, assembled on 12 April 1949, heard Lieutenant General Idwal Edwards, the Deputy Chief of Staff for Personnel, explain the genesis of the integration plan and outline its major provisions. He mentioned two major steps to be taken in the first phase of the program. First, the 332nd Fighter Wing would be inactivated on or before 30 June, and all blacks would be removed from Lockbourne. The commander of the Continental Air Command would create a board of Lockbourne officers to screen those assigned to the *all-black base*, dividing them into *three groups. The skilled and qualified officers and airmen would be reassigned worldwide to white units 'just like any other officers or airmen of similar skills and qualifications.'* General assumed that the number of men in this category would not be large. Some 200 officers and 1,500 airmen, he estimated, *would be found sufficiently qualified and proficient for such reassignment.* He added parenthetically that *Colonel Davis understood the "implications" of the new policy and intended to recommend only an individual "of such temperament, judgment, and common sense that he can get along smoothly as an individual in a white unit, and second, that his ability is such as to warrant respect of the personnel of the unit to which he is transferred."* The technically unqualified but still "usable" men would be reassigned to black service units. The staff recognized, General Edwards added, *that some Negroes were unsuited for assignment to white units for "various reasons", and had specifically authorized the retention of "this type of Negro" in black units. Finally, those who were found neither qualified nor useful would be discharged under current regulations.*

After the announcement was made, interviews were conducted to determine the compatibility of the colored officers and enlisted personnel, as they were being selected and assigned to integrated units. I had not been trained into any technical skill. Let's face it, I was a singer. All these things were taking place while I was totally unaware of the consequences. I never heard if the white airmen had to go through the same type of interviews. However, this short stay in Columbus, Ohio, did open my eyes to the fact that Negroes and whites could live and work together and use the same public accommodations. Following all the interviews and selections, I received orders to report to Okinawa, Japan.

In early September 1949, I departed Lockbourne AFB and was granted two weeks leave en route to Hamilton Field, California, which was a staging area for troops waiting for transportation overseas.

The carrier ships from that port transported troops to Hawaii, Japan and Okinawa. Since the departure time was unknown, we were restricted to travel near the base. I used that time to patronize the on-base skating rink where transit personnel could skate free. After two weeks of waiting with no indication when our troop carrier ship would depart, our uniforms needed cleaning. Khaki shirts and trousers had to be laundered. The delivery time for the base laundry was uncertain. I took this to be an opportunity to make a few dollars. The $25 that I received at the beginning of the month was gone. Dorothy had asked for money to buy shoes and Rebecca had had to have a tooth removed. I posted an announcement that one-day laundry service was available for the khaki shirts and trousers.

The barracks were equipped with washers but no dryers; however, the weather was great for drying clothes outside (with no fear of the laundry smelling of smoke and requiring re-washing as my Mom had often experienced). I would wash the uniforms in the morning and use the recreation room to shoot pool until the clothes were dry. After lunch, I would check out an electric iron from supply and finish the laundry. Helping Mom wash during my early years paid off. I had money to go to the movie (never on Sunday). Of course, I attended church service on the base.

In late September 1949, when the announcement was issued for our departure, most of the troops left the base with clean uniforms. On the first day out of the harbor, the seas were rough. A large number of the troops experienced severe seasickness. The rough water did not bother me. I later wished that it had because I spent hours in the galley washing food trays. It was midnight before I was relieved of duty.

The next day was Sunday. I attended vestibule service on board the ship. After the service was over, the Chaplain asked if anyone would be interested in singing for the services as we traveled. I volunteered and was selected along with three other fellows. For the remainder of the 14-day trip, this was my only assigned duty. Having this assignment allowed me to meet daily in the Chaplain's quarters. We prayed as we prepared the program for the daily evening services. During my first experience traveling by boat, I discovered the beauty of the Pacific Ocean at night. The stars were so bright and beautiful. I considered this as an encounter with my Father, God, who had made the night and the ocean so beautiful. There I could see what I would later experience frequently: the fingerprints of God.

After several days on the ocean and final arrival in Hawaii, I was excited because it had been announced that the troops would have liberty during the stop there. After disembarking, we Negro servicemen soon realized we were not welcome. I returned to the ship along with other Negroes after a few hours because we were subject to arrest. Comments were made that in 1949, Hawaii was more prejudiced than Mississippi. This did not bother me; I had long been conditioned to racial bias and prepared to avoid any unpleasant confrontations. After two days, we were on our way to Okinawa. The evening devotions went well, and the night before we arrived at Okinawa, our group sang, "*Ye Dry Bones.*"

Okinawa, October 1949, was still war-torn. Japanese ships bombed by the Americans were still in the harbor. The one road from Naha to Kadena was coral. The Okinawan people were recovering from severe destruction. When I arrived, the military at Kadena was drinking treated water stored in canvas bags. In the Quonset hut barracks, I slept under a net because the mosquitoes were prolific.

I was assigned to Headquarters 20th Air Force. My rank was private first class (PFC). When I reported in to the squadron I did not have a trade. Remember, I had never attended Motor Transportation School. I had gone to Lockbourne from Basic Training as a singer. That was my only assigned job with the Air Force.

When I arrived in Okinawa, I was penniless, having spent the only money I had on ship at the beginning of the trip to buy cigarettes. I was on Okinawa for over a week when a black sergeant living in the same Quonset hut asked me if I had written home to let my family know that I had arrived safely. I said no, explaining that I had spent all my money and couldn't even buy a stamp. He gave me one, and I wrote home and described the entire trip to Mom.

I reported to Master Sergeant Miner, the First Sergeant for Headquarter and Headquarters Squadron, 20th Air Force. The very first job he assigned to me was to cut the grass. I recall what S.D. Landrum had told me before leaving Alabama State Teacher's College, "You won't like the military but do what you are told to do and you will make out alright." I asked the First Sergeant where I would find the lawn mower. He said, "We don't have one." I asked him if we had a sling. He said, "No, we do not have a sling." He told me to go out there and cut the grass. Well, this was my opportunity to show that *"ATTITUDE IS EVERYTHING."* On the way from the orderly room, I discovered a rotten wooden barrel with the metal rings falling off. I took one of the rings and used a large coral rock to sharpen one edge enough to use it as a sling to cut the grass. When Master Sergeant Miner saw me, I was singing "O Danny Boy" as loud as I could and cutting the grass. At the end of the week I had cut all the grass in the squadron area. This really impressed Master Sergeant Miner, so much so that he assigned me to clean the outdoor latrines. First, he told me how he wanted them cleaned, and then explained the hygiene of cleaning to prevent transmitting disease. I followed his instructions. I was assigned guard duty and walked whatever post I was assigned to with the same good attitude, although I must confess, I was scared to death in some of those areas that they sent me to guard. It was so dark and I was told that there were Japanese military hidings in nearby caves. Those were the longest hours, and I had to walk guard duty once a week.

The 20th Air Force had a football team and I made the squad in what was really sandlot football. Half the players had no equipment. If someone was fortunate enough to have brought cleats with them to

Okinawa, he used them to great advantage. There was some grass on the playing field. We had fun and I played in two games before I sprained my ankle. The season was over before I was able to play again. I played basketball until I suffered a broken nose.

Our chapel program included both Protestant and Catholic services. The priest coached the softball team. Master Sergeant Miner was very pleased with my work. He often told me that I had a good attitude, and he really liked that. I was keeping my nose clean.

After a month, I finally received a letter from home and it wasn't long before I was getting mail regularly from other family members. In November, 1949, Master Sergeant Miner thought that I needed help to handle all the details I was assigned to do. An Okinawa gentleman became my helper which was really a joke. He spoke no English, and I spoke no Japanese. I learned sign language and taught him how to swing my sling. It was getting good use. In fact, our squadron was the envy of the others because the grass was getting cut frequently. I taught "papasan" how to clean the latrines, two wooden outhouses. One procedure called for burning the paper in the bottom of the latrine. Again, I was praised by the First Sergeant for the effort I expended to make sure those outhouses were spotless. Once the fire was started in the bottom of the latrine, we would leave the area until the burning was completed. Now that I had papasan trained, I let him clean the small outhouse on the opposite end of the squadron. I took care of the large one most frequently used. For some reason, I was called away for another detail, but before I left I told papasan to clean the small outhouse. After I finished what I was doing, I knew it was about time for papasan to burn the paper in the small outhouse. I knew he would clear the area during the burning. I went into my Quonset hut and lay down to read a comic book. It wasn't too long when Master Sergeant Miner came into the hut and asked, "Richardson, what are you doing?" I said I was waiting until the burning was completed in the small outhouse, and before I could finish he interrupted and said, "Richardson, that outhouse is on fire." He later told me that I took off running so fast that I left the comic book suspended in midair. When I got near the place, papasan was running between the two outhouses with a number 10 can of water trying to put out the fire because there was no fire department. This was very bad timing because we were in the middle of the diarrhea season. It took only 15 minutes and all that was left was a hole in the ground. This is why I have stated that a good attitude means a lot. I could have lost the only stripe I had from this incident but instead, the First Sergeant had a good laugh over it.

It wasn't long after the outhouse incident that I was called into the orderly room and the Administrative Officer wanted to know what career field I wanted to enter. I answered quickly, "I want to become an aircraft mechanic." He reviewed by records and discovered that I had completed almost two years of college. He found an aircraft and engine course located at Johnson Air Base in Japan in which I was enrolled and attended. My motivation to attend aircraft and engine school had been stimulated at Lockbourne when I had met a Technical Sergeant and asked him what kind of job he had. He answered that he was an aircraft mechanic and had earned his stripes in just over six years. I knew at that point what career field I wanted, and I committed myself to earning the rank of Technical Sergeant in the same time period as he had done it. I attended 16 weeks of aircraft and engine technical school and graduated as outstanding student with a 97% overall grade point average.

The A&E course started in January, 1950, and I arrived in Japan just before Christmas. Approaching my first Christmas away from home, I was "blue" and black all over. On Christmas Eve, 1949, I was assigned duties as charge-of-quarters, a task requiring someone to be in the orderly room to answer questions and the telephone. I was listening to the Armed Forces radio when the composition of Handel's Messiah filled the air. The music sounded like the Alabama State Teachers Choir. I cried. I was lonely and homesick. Pappie O'Neal, the school's First Sergeant was black. He did not have the out-going personality of Master Sergeant James and was not one to take matters lightly. You did what you were told or suffered the consequences. So I quickly dried my tears. After Christmas service at the Base Chapel, the mess hall presented Christmas dinner. I had never seen the amount of food they prepared for us.

When classes began the first week in January, 1950, students attended from bases throughout Japan and Okinawa. Weekends were free for recreation, and we played volleyball. I made my first visit to Tokyo and found it interesting and curious to watch the Japanese reaction when General MacArthur made his appearance. On several occasions, I noticed how the citizens honored him as a war hero. The general likewise made it clear to all allied forces that they would respect the Japanese people. Unfortunately, prejudices and discrimination still followed the American military. Black servicemen knew they were not welcome in Tokyo. It was a shame that the white servicemen taught the Japanese girls to avoid black servicemen who went to Yokohama, where the clubs had good Japanese bands and the Japanese hostesses were very kind and respected black servicemen. The General had ordered service clubs to be located in major Japanese cities, clubs that were fully equipped to assist servicemen when they were in town. One could get free services such as a haircut and uniforms cleaned and pressed within an hour. There was no excuse to appear untidy in public. The military police would report anyone – officer or enlisted personnel – found in an untidy uniform or needing a haircut. Mrs. MacArthur had the service clubs equipped with dining facilities fit to accommodate a king. At any military service club in town, a Kobe steak dinner with all the trimmings cost $5.00.

After eight weeks, my grades were on top of the other students attending the course. I had plenty of opportunity to use the discipline I had learned at Mrs. Lillie James' school. I was using the lessons learned at Sunday school to treat females with respect, in spite of the language barrier. I learned that people respond favorably when respected. The spiritual foundation established in my home was solid and, while attending school in Japan, I was able to participate in the Base Chapel programs.

While visiting Yokohama, I met Cheeico, a hostess at the Olympic Cabaret who heard me sing with the band and afterward made her acquaintance. I wasn't supposed to go on stage and sing with the Japanese band. A student attending the A&E course had heard me sing on Johnson Air Base and requested that I sing a song for the troops. The band and I worked out the music and did *A Tree in the Valley.* While I was singing, a military policeman stood directly in front of the band. He waited until I finished and took me into his office. He proceeded to write a report on me for violating an ordinance forbidding servicemen from performing on stage with the Japanese. I was unaware of the ordinance and apologized. He explained that in the past, servicemen had gone on stage and attempted to play with the band and instruments had been broken. To prevent this from occurring, the bandstand was off limits to servicemen. Again, I apologized to the military policeman. He stopped writing the report and complimented me for doing a great job. Rest assured, it never happened again. Later when I visited the Cabaret and the band played a song I knew and the troops wanted me to sing, I would sing from where I was seated. Before I completed the A&E course and during the few times I was able to visit Yokohama, Cheeico and I became very close friends. I kept in touch with her, as promised, when I returned to Okinawa.

In April 1950, after completing A&E School with honors, I returned to Okinawa. It was like stepping back in time after spending 16 weeks in Japan.

After in-processing was completed, another door of opportunity opened. I was assigned to work on the specialized maintenance crew of the Commanding General of 20th Air Force, Major General Kincaid. I was the first black airman to be assigned to this top maintenance team. The selection was based on graduating as the honor student of my A&E class and disposition.

I prayed in thanksgiving for getting that assignment. Master Sergeant Drasher and Master Sergeant Zekas were the supervisors. They had years of combat experience working on the B-17. I was so excited about being selected to work on this handpicked maintenance team. Master Sergeant Drasher trained me and I followed him closely and learned everything he taught me much faster than he had anticipated. I faithfully did whatever I was told to do. The first month, I washed the entire cowling that covered the engines.

With the chapel choir, I sang my first solo, *Savior Lead Me Lest I Stray,*" in the chapel at Okinawa, which I continued to do over the years at military chapels.

I recall the Sunday in June 1950, when the announcement was made that the North Koreans had marched against South Korea. Members of the 822nd Engineering Battalion were ordered back to their base for immediate deployment. I thought back to when I had enlisted. What if I had been selected to join the army instead of the Air Force? One soldier assigned to the 822nd Engineering Battalion, an all black unit, was shipped to Korea. I never knew if he survived the large number of casualties after their arrival in Korea.

In June 1950, I was promoted to corporal with 18 months in service, and I now had two stripes. I was so excited because my dream of obtaining the grade of technical sergeant in six years was clearly right on schedule, if not ahead.

After the Korean War started, my aircraft was used to carry supplies from Okinawa to Korea. I was not allowed to fly into a war zone because I had not attended survivor's school.

Okinawa became the launching base for B-29 bombers in support of the Korean conflict. I was fascinated by the pictures of famous names painted on the nose section of B-29 aircraft of the 19th Bombardment Wing located on Guam and the 318th from McDill Air Force Base, Tampa, that were providing air strikes against North Korea. Large numbers of tents housed the influx of aircrew members and maintenance people. The runway had to be extended to accommodate B-29 takeoffs and landings.

It was breathtaking to watch those loaded B-29s take off over the China Sea. Using full throttle, the huge birds would travel with full power and speed to the end of the runway and dip as though they would crash into the sea.

In December 1950, I was promoted to sergeant with 23 months of military service and three stripes. I was two stripes away from my goal and had four years to work for the total of five.

When I was promoted to sergeant, I was named to fly with the General when he traveled to Tokyo to meet with General MacArthur. This was a tremendous responsibility and honor. Traveling to Tokyo after months on Okinawa was like visiting the big city. My growing maturity and steadfast discipline helped, and I was where I was supposed to be when the general wanted to travel.

History will someday recall the strong positive effort General MacArthur put into establishing democracy in Japan. In August 1950, voter registration took place in the Rhyrukus Islands. I flew the mission on our B-17 to drop leaflets over the outlying islands, encouraging citizens to register and prepare to elect their governors. General McClure was military governor for the Rhyrukus Islands. I had no way of knowing that I would be selected to be an honor guard to travel with General McClure to inaugurate the newly-elected governors.

In December 1950, I attended the Bob Hope Christmas show, which had performed in Korea and came to Okinawa. Les Brown's band played and the Andrew Sisters were singers. Like future Bob Hope shows I would enjoy, that one was great. Life was good. Rather, life was great for the little boy from Jackson Street.

Just before Christmas, the base held a talent contest. I entered and won a three-minute telephone call home to Mom. But my euphoria was short lived. That telephone call came at a much needed time as I learned that my grandfather had passed away and my nephew, Jimmie, two years old, had contracted polio. Christmas 1950, on Okinawa, I sang with a combined choir at Midnight Mass, full of faith, hope, love and sadness for my family.

Master Sergeant Drasher's tour was ending and he received orders transferring him to an assignment in the states. Master Sergeant Zekas followed in less than a month. Master Sergeant Morrelli became supervisor of the general maintenance team.

After the election was over in the Rhyrukus Islands, I traveled as an honor guard by boat to the island (more than a day's travel from Okinawa) to conduct the first inauguration ceremony. The citizens of that island had never seen a black person. I became a celebrity. They wanted to touch me and feel my hair. I was 20 years old and allowed them to do so. They commented, "joto, joto", which means good.

After the inauguration ceremony was over, our return trip was delayed because of a typhoon in the China Sea. We spent a week waiting for the weather to clear up. The building where we were staying had no running water, so after a week had passed, we were beginning to smell from the heat, and nowhere to take a shower. Out of self-defense, I suspect, the officer in charge of the honor guards suggested that we go to the ocean and take a bath. Some of the team did. One of the drill team members said there was a Japanese shower house nearby. I joined them and went to get a bath. The two airmen were white. When I walked into the shower house with them, the owner caught sight of me. He had never seen a black person. After I took a seat on a stool and started washing my body, a few minutes passed and the owner came to me and offered to help bathe me. He had his own bar of soap and a small bristle brush. He rubbed and scrubbed but noticed that nothing was coming off. He looked at my arm and rubbed harder. The other guys were falling out laughing and I said, "Think he can rub it off?"

After 10 minutes, he motioned for me to step up on a stool near a large container of hot water. He made an attempt to push me into the water, but I had to react quickly. I was able to motion him off and so he left and shortly afterwards, so did we. He refused to take my money, feeling, I guess, that he had failed and I was leaving unclean. To be truthful, that was the best bath I had since my sister Rebecca had stopped bathing me, and boy, could she scrub. Felt like sandpaper.

The other two inauguration ceremonies were uneventful, and the team received a letter of appreciation from General McClure for an outstanding job. This was the first of many such letters I would receive over the years ahead.

My training as a maintenance staffer paid off as I began flying with the crew to Guam. In 1950, when I made my first trip, there was not much on Anderson Air Base but a flight line with B-29 aircraft. The flying time from Okinawa to Guam took 12 hours and every bit of fuel to cover the distance.

My last trip to Guam was August 1951. A typhoon was heading toward Okinawa and the Generals' aircraft was ordered off the island. The flight plan included a stop in the Philippines and then on to Guam. The navigator was a new second lieutenant. Master Sergeant Morrelli warned the navigator about the storm and what was needed to avoid heading into it, but the navigator assured him the flight plan took the crew out of any danger from the storm.

After a few hours in flight, we hit the storm head-on. Our B-17 was tossed all over the sky. I had taken a position in the tail section of the aircraft and it took all of Captain Oakley's expertise to prevent it from flipping over. The time seemed forever. I prayed but felt that we would not survive the strength of the storm. All at once, everything was as smooth as silk. We had entered the eye of the typhoon. It was so smooth it seemed the engines had stopped. By the time we landed at Clark Air Base, Philippines, Captain Oakley had depleted the hydraulic pressure piloting the aircraft during the storm. He landed the aircraft and discovered there was no hydraulic braking pressure; it was good that the runway was long at Clark Air Base. The story was, when the aircraft took off from Okinawa there were four whites and one black on board the aircraft. They were surprised to see five whites come out of the aircraft. I do believe that trip was the real beginning of my love for God and how to pray.

We refueled at Clark Air Base and later that night took off for Guam. Again, Master Sergeant Morrelli told the navigator that if he was not accurate about the time it took to get to Guam, we would all be swimming. The following morning we were getting low on fuel but no sign of Guam. Again, I prayed. With only fumes left in the tanks and the reserve tank nearly empty, we spotted Guam and landed uneventfully.

During leisure time, we toured the islands and, while on the trip, an aircrew member took pictures of me climbing a coconut tree. The Charlie Corn Snack Bar was the only public eating facility on the base. Our return trip was smooth. On long trips to and from Guam, everyone had a period of time at the controls of the B-17. As a sergeant, I flew the aircraft for two hours. The autopilot system was the best. All that was required was to turn a few knobs and the plane stayed on course. To think, the little boy from Jackson Street at the controls of a super flying fortress and doing a good job.

When we returned to Okinawa, we learned that two airmen had lost their lives during the typhoon. The vehicle in which they were riding had blown over in the strong winds.

The other B-17 left behind was unharmed. Technical Sergeant Burke volunteered to ride out the storm by turning the rotating propellers into the wind. That was an approved procedure to use during a typhoon and the aircraft remained safely on the island.

In September, 1951, and after two years, my tour of duty on Okinawa was ending. I would leave behind Staff Sergeant Strickland who had become my best friend during the two years I had lived as the only black airman in my Quonset hut. Bobby was the only white airman who used the word "nigger" frequently. I ignored his comments, and he never posed any threat. It was the only kind of attitude that he knew. The years ahead would be managed with the same positive attitude and discipline.

I had tested the outcome of the interview conducted at Lockbourne Air Force Base and had passed with flying colors. I had proved to be compatible to work and live in the upcoming integrated United States Air Force.

In September 1951, I was transferred from Okinawa and assigned to the Air Proving Ground Command at Eglin Air Force Base, Florida, where Jim Crow Laws were still imposed on the base. I spent three weeks of leave at home. Mom was so glad to see me. I had planned to surprise her. I had traveled from Okinawa to Hawaii without letting her know that I was on my way home. When I told a friend my plan, he discouraged that surprise because it might be too big a shock to Mom and turn out badly. I wrote a letter while on the boat and mailed it when I got to Hawaii. In Hawaii, discrimination had not changed since the first trip two years earlier. I left the boat long enough to mail my letter home.

The train ride from California to Florida was uneventful. I arrived home and found Mom sick. The doctor prescribed medication, which I purchased for her. She was so happy to have me home again.

When I returned to Pensacola from Okinawa, Chappie James had returned from Korea where he had served a tour and was shot down and rescued.

He had been promoted to captain. Besides my mother, I visited Mrs. Lillie James while I was home on leave between assignments. Chappie, at the same time, was home on leave. We shared experiences about things that had taken place from the time we left Lockbourne. He was assigned to Otis Air Force Base where he became Squadron Commander.

While shopping for a gift for Mom, I met Mrs. Dubois. She wanted to know where I had been and praised me for the way I was wearing my uniform. I was a sergeant, and had earned several ribbons for serving on the Japanese occupational forces and in the area during the Korean conflict. She explained that her niece's boyfriend was stationed in Korea, and she asked if I would come to their home and talk with Helen about that area. I agreed that I would come over.

I knew Mr. Dubois from the church and he was Mom's class leader. Helen had graduated from high school and was enrolled in junior college. We reacquainted ourselves from the early years when we had first met at vacation Bible school when she was only six years old. I shared my experiences while stationed on Okinawa but this was nothing to compare with Korea. I had nothing really to share, other than my aircraft had been used to support the efforts in Korea.

I reported to Eglin Air Force Base, was assigned to the Aircraft Maintenance Squadron and worked in the engine shop as the first black airman to work in that facility. I came to Eglin as a senior aircraft mechanic. Black airmen assigned to Eglin had been cooks, truck drivers, carpenters and base support workers. I had a hard-core skill. I was assigned to strip the engines removed from B-17s that had flown through the atomic blasts at Antaweetoc in the Pacific. Mr. Cunningham, my supervisor, was a good man.

I was not told directly to use the latrine in the hangar, but I refused. I would wait until I returned to the barracks. The same was true with regards to the drinking fountain. Again, I would wait until I returned to the squadron to drink water. The base was segregated. Black airmen had their barracks below Eglin Parkway. We had our own BX, chapel, dining hall and club. There really was no reason to go north of Elgin Parkway after dark.

I had been working in the engine shop for two months when the shop received a power pack to build an R-4360 engine for a B-36 aircraft. I had never seen a power pack that large. I went into the area where the mechanics were putting the engine into its stand. It stood almost to the ceiling of the hanger. When I entered the area I heard a voice say, "Get out of this area you black son-of-a-bitch." I stayed put because I couldn't believe what I was hearing. He said it again, "Get out of this area you black son-of-a-bitch." He came forth appearing to be angry, and I left the area. That was a time when I had to use the power of prayer and self-control. I had witnessed a similar incident when one of the neighbors had verbally attacked Mom. She was degraded in a very insulting way. I stood and listened to it all. Mom never returned a word. Of course, it was obvious she was hurt deeply. Now I was hurt to think someone, without reason, would call my Mom a "bitch." I prayed and I promised myself that someday I would prove to that man I was not the son of a bitch. My first reaction was to strike back. I could have because I was in good physical condition. But instead, I recalled what I learned in elementary school. This was a door of opportunity. Although it was unacceptable, in bitter reality, I knew if I entered that door, and left it open, it would help other black airmen who would someday come along behind me. My love for my Mom was gravely attacked. I knew to take revenge would cause a serious problem. Depressed, I left the area with my heart hurting. This was a tremendous test of managing raw prejudices. I discovered that I was equipped spiritually to handle present and upcoming situations. For instance, when the engine shop would have cookouts, I could not attend. I was handed $5.00 to go and celebrate alone.

For Christmas, December 1951, I visited my grandmother in Beatrice. My grandfather had passed away while I was stationed in Okinawa. The visit was good. Before I left Pensacola for Beatrice, Johnnie Mae and I had agreed to remain friends because she had entered into another relationship while I was stationed in Okinawa.

When I returned from visiting grandma, I called Helen and asked if she would like to go to a movie. She got permission, and this was our first date. Neither of us was serious. Helen's boyfriend was in Korea and I didn't want to do anything to disturb that relationship.

On April 1, 1952, one of the white airmen came and told me that I had been promoted to Staff Sergeant. I strongly suggested that this was a practical joke, and I did not respond. April fool's day is a horrible time to be told you've been promoted. I waited until midnight when everyone was asleep and sneaked out of the barracks to read the bulletin board where the promotions were posted and, sure enough, my name was on the list. Finally, with three years of service, I had been promoted to staff sergeant. I had one more stripe to make and I would be technical sergeant with five stripes and three years to go.

I had planned only to stay in the Air Force for three more years to help Dorothy complete college. The three years had passed and Dorothy still had another year to go. I reenlisted for another three years to continue helping her.

At that point, I had started working at the Officer's Club at Eglin and the income really helped. An allotment was going to Mom to help with Dorothy and whatever else Mom needed money for.

Mr. Pierce, foreman of the engine shop observed my positive attitude and removed me from those contaminated engines and offered me a promotion if I took the job in the tool crib. I took the assignment and Mr. Pierce kept his promise with my promotion to staff sergeant. The position and promotion did not remove me from contact with the person who had called me a black-son-of-a-bitch. Whenever he came to the tool crib, he would yell out "boy" and would request what he wanted. This drew laughs from the whites hearing how he called out to me. When he would use an electrical cord, he was required to roll the cord up before returning it. He would bring the unwrapped cord back and call to me to pick it up and wrap it. I did. This continued until the transfer I had requested came through.

As 1952 arrived, I purchased an automobile and could come to Pensacola regularly when I was not working. I was seeing Helen frequently, and we were getting to know each other better.

I had completed three years of military service and had earned four stripes. Meanwhile, my faith and love for God were growing steadily. On the weekends, I took up where I had left off – attending and singing in the choir at Allen Chapel Church. There were times the Pastor would call on me to pray. Mom was touched when she listened to me leading the prayer. She had come to that time in life when the burdens she had experienced turned to tears of joy and victory. She was a great proponent of turning the other cheek. For me, life was changing and with it were opportunities to succeed or fail. There were no shades of gray. I had to be on guard against the biggest evil: wasting time.

I had my first experience of living outside the United States and a long way from Jackson Street, and out of the shadow of my Mom. I found it extremely important to use time to develop self-discipline. I helped others and worked hard to prevent idle time, which Mom always said, was the devil's workshop. I was beginning to realize that I was helping make a difference in the racial merge taking place in the United States Air Force. This little boy from Jackson Street had participated as an honor guard in organizing the first democratic election and inauguration to take place in Okinawa and had, likewise, played an important part in General MacArthur's occupational forces by promoting good will between the Japanese people and Americans. I had used my gift of singing to promote good will and had learned that singing is a universal language.

The ensuing years were vital in helping to develop human relations and social justice at Eglin Air Force Base in 1951, when segregation was still being practiced. Another door of opportunity would open as I worked part-time at Eglin Air Base Officer's Club. The job put me in touch with all the Air Proving Ground Commanders. I was headwaiter and took care of all the Commanding General's special parties at the club and at his quarters.

General Timberlake had replaced General Boatner, and Mrs. Timberlake was a perfect hostess. She relied on me to make sure her private parties were properly organized. I took real good care of all of these special functions. I felt I could make a real difference from this vantage point.

Back Home To:
Love, Marriage, Baby Carriage . . .

and Race Relations

When I returned from Okinawa, in September 1951, I learned, after talking with Johnnie Mae, that she had entered into another relationship. Although our romantic relationship ended, we remained friends. Perhaps I should have felt hurt emotionally, yet I knew deep down within me that I would always remain in touch with her family because Mrs. Malden and I had grown close to each other. Mr. Malden was extremely quiet and never talked very much with anyone. He loved his family and was very concerned about the boys who dated his three daughters. I considered myself extremely fortunate because he was friendly and kind to me. I never wanted to do anything that would cause any concern about my dating his daughter. I definitely wanted to remain close to the Malden family because they were the very first family which had openly accepted me. It was obvious from the unfavorable treatment I had experienced from others that they were definitely different. Johnnie Mae and I ended our relationship during the Christmas holiday season of 1951. I purchased a gift and gave it to her.

Instead of spending that Christmas with her, I spent it with my grandmother in Beatrice. I had been overseas on Okinawa when my grandfather died and since I was unable to attend the funeral, this was a chance to spend time with her and other family members. After only a few days, I returned home and, it occurred to me, I had not spoken to Helen during the Holidays, so I gave her a call. She sounded as though she was pleased to hear from me. We talked for a while and since it was in the early afternoon, I asked if I could come and visit. She said yes. When I arrived, it was early, and I asked if she would go to the movie with me. She was granted permission from her parents, and we went out together on our very first date.

I had often heard of the long-range vision of God and, unknowingly, I was entering into one of those visions. It was not my intent to get involved with a long-term relationship with Helen because I knew that there was an age difference between us, and I felt that she was much too young for me to be dating her.

I also knew she had a boyfriend whom she had met while attending boarding school in Anne Mammy, Alabama. He was stationed in Korea. It was for this reason that I first visited the Dubois' to try and shed some light on what I may have known about the military situation in Korea. Helen was very honest when she spoke to me about her love relationship with him, and I appreciated knowing so that I would not interfere with that romantic liaison at all. She admitted that she was writing to him frequently. I strongly encouraged that because I had first-hand experience of how important letters were when I was overseas and knowing the dangerous situation that he was in, I did not want to interrupt that communication. However, we began seeing each other frequently as the months went by and Mr. and Mrs. Dubois did not object. Our families had grown up worshiping at Allen Chapel AME church and her parents accepted the fact that Helen and I were seeing each other. It was obvious that the Dubois' were not as open and friendly as the Malden's. Mrs. Dubois placed strict rules regarding the time we spent together – something that the Malden's had not done when I was dating Johnnie Mae. Even without restrictions, Johnnie Mae and I would not go very far from their home whenever I did visit her. I would walk her home from school when we were both attending Booker T. Washington High School. Johnnie Mae was in the same class as Dorothy. She was two years behind me in high school; however, Mrs. Dubois insisted that wherever we went we had to be back at home before 9 p.m. during the week and 10 p.m. on the weekend. I agreed with the restrictions because Helen was a student at the time attending Washington Junior College. Because of the personal feelings within, and realizing the age span, combined with how I perceived the coolness of Mr. and Mrs. Dubois, I never felt completely comfortable visiting Helen. I really considered her much too young for me to be dating. Somehow, the age difference did not concern her. Even with the preconceived thoughts, our friendship was growing but not to the extent that it would make it difficult or impossible for her to reestablish her romantic relationship with her present boyfriend whenever he would return from Korea.

In November 1951, prior to the Christmas holidays, I had gained employment at the Eglin Officer's Club as a waiter. The small income from the Air Force was not enough for me to provide the money that my sister Dorothy needed to complete her college education. On some weekends I worked at the club but did not come into Pensacola. On those weekends that I remained at Eglin, I became actively involved with the Base Chapel Program.

On one occasion, I was requested to sing with a visiting band, which was playing at the Officer's Club. The Base Chaplain was there at the time I was singing and, after the song was over, he approached me and asked if I would come and sing during the service some weekend. I accepted his invitation. I remember singing "Let Us Break Bread Together." Thereafter, I was called on to sing whenever I was available. The association with the Chapel program, plus the recognition I was gaining at the Officer's Club combined with the positive attitude doing my job at the engine shop was extremely helpful toward my promotion to staff sergeant.

While I was growing up in the neighborhood on Jackson Street, I was being prepared by God to be a part of a larger effort during the struggle to bring about integration in the military. Even with every reason to be indifferent toward my white brother, my heart was structured by God to be open and to share the real experience of what living the Christian life was all about. I learned in the midst of all the racial bitterness that existed at that time that I could make a difference. I could accept the good with the bad. I could accept the fact that working harder and doing the unpleasant jobs were all a part of God's plan to change the minds and hearts of those who strongly opposed Negroes and never desired for black people to live in or be in their environment.

After working at the Officer's Club for a short period of time, I was called upon to serve at the Commanding General's private parties. General Boatner was the commander of the Air Proving Ground Command. He entertained important men and women that he considered would be helpful in promoting air power. He hosted what was known as the Joint Civilian Orientation Conference (JCOC) and presented an air-power demonstration, which included the most modern developed weapons, as well as the latest version of aircraft that were designed and capable of delivering the ordinance, which was being developed primarily at Eglin Air Force Base.

I later learned that what I was doing as a simple waiter was contributing to what would later become the largest Air Force Base in the United States and the world's leader in developing and testing conventional warheads. This also gave me the opportunity to serve very important business people, as well as educators and early pioneers of the future U.S. Air Force's air power. My talents as a waiter and the positive attitude I exhibited when working around white people were quick to gain their attention. In all that was going on in my life, I was constantly in prayer. I employed the teaching I had learned from my home, school and church in all my activities. I was clearly a part of Mrs. Lilly James' vision that someday the door of opportunity would open and you needed to keep your bags packed to enter whenever and wherever that door opened for you.

To overcome adversities, I used my Christian training to avoid resentment when criticized and rejected. When I would go into Pensacola, I would attend my church. Mom was so proud of the manner in which I was conducting my affairs. I was remaining true to my commitment to not do anything that would bring any embarrassment to her. She had made great sacrifices for us. Church members were aware of my love for Mom and how I showed respect for others. I knew in my heart what it would take to prove that what she had done would not be in vain. We maintained our deep love and affection for each other. Although Helen's parents attended Allen Chapel, she no longer attended because she had converted to Catholicism.

I had worked tough jobs, accepted racial slurs and still maintained my composure. I wanted to succeed and I was willing to do what it took while still avoiding doing things that I knew were against the

Commandments of God and any misconduct that would embarrass my mother. I had a goal in mind to make Mrs. Lillie James, as well as Mr. Nick Williams, proud of me. They, too, had prepared me for the difficult times ahead. I had feared facing the racial differences initially because I was keenly aware of the consequences should I cross "wrongly" over the path of white men.

While conscious of potentially unfavorable results, I moved cautiously into the future and came upon many roadblocks, aware that those blockages were placed there to observe my reactions. Yet I faced them and went where I knew I could find consolation. I found quiet moments in the Base Chapel, and I prayed a lot, cried a lot, and I wondered if I was really doing God's will or was I seeking self-gratification. I wanted more than ever to do God's will and let the future be in his Almighty Hands. I remembered what Mom had gone through on Jackson Street, but she never failed to be in church on Sunday, and she continued to remind me the "Lord is My Shepherd" and that I had an infinite *friend in Jesus*. I was learning that Jesus was always near and that prayer never fails.

In May 1952, Helen's boyfriend returned home from Korea and I deliberately stayed away from visiting or telephoning Helen to allow them the opportunity to reunite. Lo and behold, I was invited along with a few others to attend a welcome home beach party that Mrs. Dubois had planned for him. Johnson Beach, where the party was held, was designated as the colored people beach and it was located approximately 15 miles west of Pensacola near the Alabama State line. The beach was beautiful with the same snow-white sand as the white people's Pensacola Beach, which was segregated. Helen introduced me to him and he was a very fine young man. I would have ended the visits with Helen at that point had she wanted me to do so. Instead she explained to him at an appropriate time that she had entered into another relationship. He spent only a couple of days in Pensacola and then departed to his home in Michigan. Helen told me after he departed that he did not appear angry, did not question her as to who his competition was, and he did not care to know whom it was nor what had happened to their romance. She later explained to me that she considered his reaction as very positive and to some extent supportive.

Months passed after he departed and before Helen and I resumed seeing each other, although now at a different level. I fully realized the seriousness of Helen's decision to choose seeing me and removing herself from the long romantic relationship she had shared with him. I seriously focused on the fact that I had long ago committed myself to respect for females. I would do whatever I had to do to gain Helen's respect and to assure her that she had not made a mistake by allowing herself to become more deeply involved with me.

I knew the feelings I had experienced when Johnnie Mae had shared her new-found love affair with me months earlier. I had been hurt and I knew it had been difficult for Johnnie Mae to tell me what had happened. Now, I found myself on the other side of a relationship that had existed for several years. I knew in my heart that Helen had fallen in love with me. I prayed that I would live up to her expectations knowing full well that she had much on her mind as she was studying hard and trying to maintain her highly-achieved grade point average. She had graduated as valedictorian of her class in 1951, and now she was into her second year in a junior college. She did not need a relationship that would divide her attention and cause her grades to suffer. I would call and talk with her as often as I could while at the base and plan time for us to spend together whenever I was able to come into Pensacola. We arranged our dating to conform to Mrs. Dubois's strict rules.

After I was promoted to Staff Sergeant, I had purchased a car and had also reenlisted because my sister Dorothy had not completed her college education. Helen and I could go to the beach along with friends whenever I had time off. All during these years, I continued to look at Jean and Eloise, my Jackson street friends, as my sisters. They were invited to join Helen and me whenever we planned a beach trip. It was mostly on Sunday afternoons during the summer months that we planned our beach parties. Spending much of my free time with Helen became extremely enjoyable.

With deep respect, we would write letters to each other as we laid foundation for what was to come. I wanted to be the gentleman that Helen and her parents expected me to be. I would share the tempo of our relationship with Mom, and I could detect the warmest reaction in Mom's eyes that I was moving in the direction she had foreseen that I would someday marry and have a good family. When Dorothy came home from college, she would join in the fun and activities we planned together. Dorothy had become a friend of Helen's when they were younger and attending Allen Chapel. Helen claims she knew Dorothy long before she knew me. She only knew that Dorothy had a big brother.

Rebecca did not get involved with what was taking place during that time. She had two children: Gloria Jean, who was in elementary school who had attended Mrs. Lillie James' school following the family tradition. Dorothy loved Gloria and took care of her whenever she was home from college. Jimmie, Rebecca's oldest son was suffering from polio. He had become sick while I was on Okinawa and had undergone several serious surgeries. I would give Rebecca a ride to visit him in the hospital. From observing Rebecca, I learned of the deep compassion she had in her heart. This was a tremendous change from her behavior and attitude while she was growing up. Mom's prayers had been answered and now the time had come when Rebecca had responsibilities of her own. Papa dear, our stepfather, a Bahamian, deeply loved Jimmie. He would visit Jimmie in the hospital and do whatever he could to bring him comfort. Papa dear, a Catholic, showed his affection for Helen the very first time he met her when she told him she, too, was Catholic. He had met Johnnie Mae but Helen was definitely his favorite.

In the months after her previous boyfriend left, Helen and I began to become more attached. Helen and I enjoyed trips together to Eglin Air Force Base, to Mobile, Alabama to watch Mardi Gras, several beach parties with friends and I began to attend Catholic Masses. In December 1952, I proposed to Helen. The setting was not as romantic as I would have hoped it to be, but I did my best. At first, I didn't think I could approach Mr. Dubois, so I started with Mrs. Dubois. She talked for almost an hour. Then she told Mr. Dubois who ordinarily talked slowly and so I had another hour of listening to what marriage was all about. Helen had arranged for us to attend midnight Mass and the time was moving on fast and the lectures were still going on. After two and one half hours, I was granted permission to become engaged to Helen. This was Christmas Eve, 1952, when I proposed to Helen.

As I mentioned earlier, things never remain the same. I had met Helen during vacation bible school when she was only six years old. We grew up attending Allen Chapel AME Church. It was after she had finished high school in 1951 that she was granted permission to take instructions and became a Catholic. I had attended Mass with her during the time we were dating, but never a Pontifical High Mass. We arrived at church early and Helen had plenty of time to introduce me as her fiancée.

The most important individual I was introduced to was Mrs. Claudia Waters, Helen's godmother. It was Mrs. Waters who had attracted her to the Catholic faith. When Helen was small and attending elementary school near Mrs. Waters' house, Helen would call for Mrs. Waters to escort her across the busy Cervantes Street. Those moments together touched Helen deeply. Helen later explained how much she loved Mrs. Waters, and she knew back then that Mrs. Waters was Catholic. She made a commitment that when she became old enough she, too, would join the Catholic Church. While she was still in grade school, she asked her parents if she could become a Catholic. Her dad promised that when she was older, and if she still had the same feeling, he would consider it then but, for the time being, she would have to continue to worship at Allen Chapel.

As time drew near to the start of midnight Mass, I questioned why anyone would want to go to church that late at night. The Christmas setting was simply beautiful. The candles and decorations brought out the true spirit of Christmas. The manger was empty. At the entrance of the Mass during the procession, the infant child, Jesus, was brought in and placed in the manger. Earlier, the choir had sung Christmas carols. I could at that moment picture Mr. Nick Williams my Sunday school teacher sharing his Christmas story that he told every year when I was growing up at Allen Chapel church. I felt a closeness to God as I listened even though I did not understand Latin. Having always been one to get to bed early, plus that late hour and the warmth of the church along with the quiet moments caused me to fall asleep. Helen was somewhat embarrassed and poked me in the side. Startled, I sprung up in fright and, after seeing all the smoke in the church, I started rushing out of the pew. Helen restrained me. I was unaware of the large amount of incense used during the Mass and my first thoughts were that the church was on fire and that Helen was waking me up to get out of there. Looking back at those years, I can truly say the fingerprints of God were all over what was taking place. Extremely grateful, I truly know that God knows best.

Today, April 2007, we are only a month away from having been together 54 years. It was May 20, 1953 at the altar of St. Joseph Church in Pensacola, Florida, that Helen and I exchanged our wedding vows. It was a moment in time that I will forever remember. It was three in the afternoon. That entire day, up until the time we stood at that altar, appeared to be special. I could feel the presence of God and now it was time to accept this new challenge. I recall sweating more in those 15 minutes than ever before. The little boy off of Jackson Street was entering into a life commitment more challenging than anything he had ever dreamed of.

During that ceremony, as Father Ruddy questioned if I would accept children freely and bring them up in the teaching of the church. I answered, "yes." He asked if I would love Helen in good times and in sickness and health until death do us part? I answered "yes." In silence I added "with the help of God." I knew at that moment I had to depend upon my heavenly Father to live out the promises I had made. The other mental thought was my ability to so do. Again, I said to myself "yes." What I learned over the years was that God keeps secrets better than anyone I know. The future would depend on how well I would live out the promises I had made. **That was a very important day in my life.** This was the second time Mom cried because of my accomplishment. The first time was after graduation in 1947, and now I was fulfilling a dream she had shared with me. She said she wanted me to get married and have a family and to be a good father to my children. She had explained how she wanted to provide a home for us with the kind of support she knew from her grandparents. As I passed by Mom while processing out of the church, our eyes caught each other's. I could see tears but beyond those tears was a sign of joy and best wishes. Even though she had married Papa Dear, it was late in life and not as she had hoped, although Papa Dear was a good man and he really loved Mom and us children.

Our wedding reception was well prepared by Mr. Golden and most of our family and friends attended. It was a great feeling standing next to Helen, and she looked beautiful as we cut the wedding cake. The photographer took a great picture, which hangs in a special place on the wall in our family room. The following day, May 21, 1953, we departed for New Orleans where we spent a week-long honeymoon.

When we returned to Elgin Air Force Base to our first apartment on base, I learned that the Officer's Candidate School (OCS), which I had applied for, had reduced its enrollment and, if I was still interested, I could reapply in September 1953. Helen and I had planned our wedding based on a time frame that would have allowed me to attend OCS. By September 1953, Helen was expecting our first child and I declined reapplying for OCS. The first months of marriage required a tremendous amount of adjusting. Our neighbors, Gloria and Henry Burrell were Catholics, and they offered to give Helen a ride to Mass on Sundays. I would leave at a different time to attend my services on base.

Things had not changed much with regard to integration on base. Before Helen and I were married, I was not invited to attend any of the social functions of the engine shop or the squadron. After marriage, I was offered $5.00 to stay away from the functions and to use the money to take Helen somewhere else to eat.

Our other friends were, Thomasine, Jake, Shorty, Bill and Catherine, and the Warfield's. On weekends we would gather at the NCO club in the all-black section of the base. Bands from Pensacola entertained us. Girls were brought on base from Fort Walton Beach, Crestview and DeFuniak Springs. Gambling was authorized downtown and on base.

The time working on the flight line and part time at the officer's club left Helen alone most of the days through the week. To spend time with Helen I tried to avoid working on the weekends at the officer's club although that was the best time for making tips. She grew bored and lonely but when we were together, she had a time adjusting to my humor. I enjoyed playing tricks on her. She totally resented it. For several weekends she would pack her luggage to leave and go back home. Somehow, I would soothe the situation and we would unpack the luggage. She was pregnant, and I did not understand all the morning sickness she was going through. Together we worked our way through those months of pregnancy.

Mid January Walter Harold Richardson II was born. I received the call at three o'clock in the afternoon that Helen was going into the delivery room. I was working on a T-33 aircraft. When I got the message, I rushed to the hospital. The nurse stopped me short of entering the delivery room. I was greasy and over excited. Shortly after I arrived, Helen delivered. I was invited back to the nursery. I was overtaken with joy as I looked at this newly born baby being held in the nurse's arms. I visited Helen and she was so tired. I left to spread the news in my squadron that I was a dad. My neighbors were happy for me. Later than evening I was able to hold Walter. Helen was more alert, and we both shared our joy.

Before Walter was born, Helen was given a dog, but André and I didn't get along well. When Helen was admitted into the hospital, I shut André out of the house. Helen was discharged on Sunday, January 1954. I had prepared a big meal. She asked, "Who did the cooking?" I said, "I did." All these months I had withheld letting Helen know I was a cook. She wanted to know where André was. I said he was outside somewhere. When he appeared, he was dirty and appeared to be sick. I took him to the vet the following day. The first night Walter (now called Rickey) was home, he cried a lot. I later learned that he was hungry. Helen was obeying some guidelines she had received from the doctor's office. Finally, I increased his formula, and he was okay. The day after Rick was born seemed so long on the flight line. I wanted so much to be home with them. He was a great baby. I thanked God for him and asked that I be provided with as much love for him as I had experienced as a baby. I recalled the promise I had made to receive children lovingly and to bring them up in the teaching of the church. I felt ready to live up to that commitment.

During that year, the Supreme Court outlawed segregated schools. Sometime after the decision, Major General Timberlake hosted a general conference at Eglin where all of the four-star generals of the Air Force came to outline future strategy for that branch. With my security clearance, I was the waiter selected to take care of them. I met Generals Hoyt, Vanderburg, Twining, LeMay, Norstad, Stratemeyer, Rawlings, Partridge and Weyland. Since General Norstad arrived early, I was assigned to prepare his breakfast after which the general asked if I had time to talk for a while. I said, "yes." He wanted to know the reactions of the black community with regard to the Supreme Court decision. I said that I had not noticed any reactions of a victory won. I went on to say that most people I talked with wanted to wait and see how the white people would react. It took the schools in Fort Walton 10 years to react. General Norstad told me about one of his assignments during which he wanted a black orderly on his staff. Stationed in North Carolina, he said that he contacted city officials and asked if they had any objections dealing with a black male and they had none. He said North Carolina was the first to start school integration. We talked about the Air Force and what the future might portend. We spent over an hour together, and I left that meeting uplifted that I would be a part of our air power. This was my fifth year in the Air Force. I reenlisted for an additional three years because Dorothy had not yet completed college. One of the waitresses was highly impressed with General LeMay. She asked if I would get his autograph for her. I took a note pad and approached General LeMay and asked for his autograph and pointed out the young lady wanted it. He smiled, something very unusual for him, and signed the pad for me.

When the conference was over, General Norstad requested I meet him at his quarters. When I arrived, he asked me to help with his packing. When I finished, the staff car was waiting for him. As his car departed I gave him a snappy salute. Several times after that, whenever General Timberlake would attend other conferences, General Norstad would send his best wishes. I learned later from Colonel Blackwell, General Norstad had visited military personnel and reviewed my records. When he learned that Helen and I had a young baby, he changed his mind about taking me back to France with him. He was commander of Supreme Headquarters, Allied Personnel Europe (SHAPE).

After promotion to staff sergeant I was transferred to the Aircraft Repair Squadron and I worked for Master Sergeant Roberts. The move from the tool crib in the engine shop was to allow me to train for upgrade to seven level, thereby making me eligible for promotion to technical sergeant.

Rick was growing, and Helen and I enjoyed him so much. I had André to deal with as well. Rick and André became good friends. It took over a week to get Rick back to normal whenever we visited Pensacola. Mom and the Dubois' would let him do whatever he wanted to do. I couldn't believe it was the Lilly that I grew up with. A month after Rick was born, he was baptized at St. Joseph Church where Helen and I had been married. Mrs. Waters was the godmother

Work on the flight line was going well. The white civilians were making adjustments to accept me, but 1954 was not an easy year for colored airmen at Eglin. One airman left the colored squadron and went to the main Base Exchange to get a hair cut. The barber refused to cut his hair. The incident provoked the news media to come to Eglin.

After that incident, things began to change. Black officers visiting Eglin resided with other black families. The NCO Club began serving black airmen and their families. In 1955, I achieved my seven-level making me eligible for promotion to technical sergeant. With six years in service, I was on course with the goal that I had set for myself. When the white staff sergeants learned that I had achieved my seven-level, they began to study to get theirs. The main reason the white airmen would not try and get a seven-level was because they would then be eligible for transfer. Most of them loved the area. Fishing and hunting were very good.

Helen and I had not yet gained the recognition to be included in their squadron functions. Rick was a year old and walking. He loved the beach and on weekends when I was off duty, Helen and I would take him there. The single lane area along Highway 98 was bare. The sand was snow white and the emerald-colored waves were beautiful. A fisherman could catch as many fish as he wanted from the shore of the beach.

Our closest friends were the Burrell's. Helen would ride to church with them. Still a Methodist, I would keep Rick while Helen was at Mass. I really enjoyed my time with him. Bill and Katherine Smack were our neighbors. Helen and Katherine became very close friends. Katherine was from Bermuda.

At that time, Helen told me she was pregnant with our second child. The baby was due in December 1955. I was happy about the news and I wondered if the love God had supplied for Helen and Rick was sufficient to share with one more? Well, the answer to that was about to be learned. Four of the staff sergeants who had refused to get a seven level did get awarded and promoted afterward. Although I was eligible when I was awarded my seven level, I was not promoted ahead of the white sergeants.

At the end of November 1955, I was called into Captain Dean's office. He asked if Helen had had her baby yet? I said, "no." He said, "You told us that the baby was due in November. I agreed but it hasn't arrived yet. Captain Dean said that one other sergeant had a new baby and that he had been promoted to master sergeant. I responded and said that was nice. He asked again, "Are you sure Helen has not had her baby?" I said not unless it had happened while I was here at work, and I was sure my neighbors would have called to let me know. Then he said,

"You have really messed up the system." I asked "How?" He said, "You were promoted to technical sergeant and your wife has not had the baby. Then he stood up extended his hand and congratulated me. He told me that the promotion list was being prepared in the Orderly Room and for me to go and get my copy. There were others near the door when Captain Dean made the announcement. They, too, congratulated me. Master Sergeant Roberts was very proud of me. Unless I would find out differently, I was the very first black aircraft mechanic to be promoted in that squadron. Assigned to the evening shift, I was granted the rest of the evening off. I went and bought my new stripes and took them to Katherine and asked her to sew them on for me. With them on my uniform, I went home. On the way I prayed to God in thanksgiving. I had achieved my goal. I had over six years in the Air Force and I was promoted to technical sergeant. This was indeed a great achievement because there were black airmen retiring who had only reached the grade of staff sergeant.

When I arrived home, Helen wanted to know why I was not working. She, too, had been waiting for my promotion. When I entered the house with my new stripes on, she didn't recognize them. I brushed up against her, but she never paid any attention to my sleeves. Finally, I had to tell her that I had been promoted. She was so happy and excited that her labor started. In just a couple of days later in early December, Wayne Patrick Richardson was born. I called Captain Dean and told him I was now in order. Helen and I purchased our first home in a new all-black subdivision in Fort Walton Beach. We were not completely settled in place when Wayne arrived. With my new promotion came additional duties. I was assigned On-the-Job Trainer (OJT) for the section and also assigned the duties as a crew chief, which modified aircraft for non-nuclear delivery. One white mechanic went to the officer in charge and told the civilian foreman that he was not going to work for a *nigger*. Captain Dean happened to overhear the complaint. He told the man "either you work for Technical Sergeant Richardson or you can consider yourself fired." He returned to work and did what he was told to do.

One of the assignments that I had was to remove the oxygen systems from the C-124 cargo aircraft. One day when all the work was done, four of us sat down and began to play penny poker. We were making our bets when Warrant Officer McDowell came on board and caught us gambling. I was in the midst of it. A few minutes later Master Sergeant Roberts came on board the aircraft and said that it had been reported to the front office that gambling was going on inside the aircraft and that when the culprits were identified, they would be busted. Fear washed over me. I had just been promoted and now, I was about to lose these hard-earned stripes over a silly game of poker. At the close of the day, I was ready to go in and turn myself in as one of the players. When I walked into the office to tell Mr. Holloway about the gambling, he asked, "Richardson how are you doing on the C-124?" I reported that all the oxygen system was now removed. I started to tell him I was the one who had been gambling when he spoke up and said. "Thanks and have a good evening." I prayed all the way home.

I had to tell Helen what had happened, and I was sure that in the morning I would get the axe. Rick lifted my spirits with some funny routine he performed for me. In fact, every time I would return from work, Rick would do a five-minute act for me. Wayne, now being called Pat, was the sweetest baby to be sure, but he had not yet accepted his new brother. When we had arrived home with him, Rick had thrown a shoe into the bassinet. However, this jealousy didn't last long. Rick began teaching Pat all of his dirty tricks. I became aware of the additional portion of love God had granted me. Now I had the four and I had more than sufficient love for all.

Shortly after the gambling incident, I was told that Mr. Nadicksbernd wanted me to become a Quality Control Inspector for aircraft engines. Captain Dean approved the transfer. Since I had the responsibility for on-the-job training, there were records which had to be updated before I departed the section. For two weeks I worked updating all the training records. When they were all completed, I reported to Captain Dean. He asked me to be seated. When I sat down, I noticed that Mr. Holloway, Master Sergeant Roberts and Master Sergeant Dietrich gathered in the office. Captain Dean said, "Richardson, I have one last request. "What is it, sir?" He said please leave your poker cards because there are other people here who would like to play. I was so shocked and they all had a big laugh over it. They even spoke of times when they had been caught gambling. Master Sergeant Robert, my main supporter said, "We knew it was you Richardson and in our car pool we would not let you in on it. I told him how I had come in to confess my guilt but no one was interested in hearing me. They all congratulated me on my new assignment, and we all left the office laughing. Once again, a positive attitude paid off. There were many times when I felt that I would not make it. I was the only black sergeant in the group, and I knew there was jealousy and each day could be the one that would take me down. I prayed a lot during those months and years.

Mr. Brandley and Mr. Nadicksbernd were members of St. Mary's Catholic Church. I felt that they had seen me there in the audience. Mr. Brandley was a great person and Mr. Ferguson, my supervisor, was a Baptist. When Mr. Ferguson learned I was to be a new Catholic convert, he would question me about some of the things we believed in but I was not able to answer his questions. I knew he was in the car pool with his boss, Mr. Brandley, so I suggested he pose those questions to Mr. Brandley. I got no more questions and I was assigned as a Quality Control Inspector in the Engine Shop. It turned out I would have to inspect the completed work of the man, the one who had called me a black S.O.B. in 1951. So, I would have the opportunity to show forth my mother's attitude. I knew how to turn the other cheek. Every time I inspected one of his engines, I always complimented him. He seldom acknowledged my remarks. One Saturday I received a call from this man requesting and engine inspection. This was a very high priority project so I went to the engine shop to inspect the engine. He met me at the hangar door and apologized that the engine was not really ready. I accepted his apology and he offered to buy me a cup of coffee while I was waiting. Even though I was not a coffee drinker I accepted because the invitation was coming from him, so we went together to the flight line snack bar. After a couple of hours, the engine was completed, and I inspected it and did not find anything that was hard to correct. He thanked me and again apologized for keeping me so long. ***Thanks, Mom***

Since our move Helen had been unable to make her church services. I was directing the choir at Gregg Chapel AME church in Fort Walton and one Sunday an argument broke out about what color the inside of the church should be painted. I had Rick at church with me that Sunday. Emotions got hot, and I excused myself. I returned home and told Helen that I was going to join the Catholic Church. Looking for a great leap of joy I was surprised when Helen kept on doing whatever it was she was doing and said, "That's nice." I contacted Father McGuire at Eglin Air Force Base and asked to take instructions. He referred me to Monsignor Cunningham, Pastor of St. Mary's Church in Fort Walton Beach. I took private instructions from Father McHume. On June 2, 1957, in a private ceremony, I was re-conditionally baptized into the Catholic Church. If history were researched, it would reveal that I was the first African-American convert for St. Mary's Church up to 1957. I know that when I started attending Mass in that parish, there were no other black people worshiping there. The following week, after I was baptized, I heard the announcement on Sunday that each Monday a devotion to the Blessed Mother was being held. I attended, and it was there that I became acquainted with the Mother of my God, Mary Most Holy. I learned how to pray the rosary. Mr. Joe Barranco worked with me in quality control. I had a great devotion to the Blessed Mother, and he taught me about the rosary. Over the years Monsignor Cunningham accepted me as one of his favorite people.

Our neighbors around our new home were Lieutenant Smith and Mildred, Captain Franklin and Gladys, Sergeant Lester Folk, Pee Wee Taylor, Mr. and Mrs. McKinnie, Mr. and Mrs. Dowdell, Lieutenant Earnest and Jean Clayton. Mom was so proud of us. She cosigned the loan for us to be able to purchase this home. Helen loved flowers, and had a beautiful garden. We entertained ourselves in that community. We played a lot of different card games and monopoly. We would catch large bags of blue crabs out of the Sound on Highway 98.

During the summer of 1957, we planned our vacation to travel down to Miami, Florida. We went down the Gulf side and planned to return up the Atlantic coast. We spent one night in Miami, staying in the famous black St. John Hotel. This was where all the black stars such as Nat King Cole, Ella Fitzgerald and other well-known entertainers stayed when they went to Miami. Rick wanted to swim in the pool. But all that I had were G.I. khaki trunks. I discouraged him. Our return trip was uneventful.

Shortly after we returned, Helen said she was pregnant again. Major General Timberlake had transferred and Major General Robert Burns had replaced him as the Air Proving Ground Commander. General and Mrs. Burns had not been assigned long before I was introduced to him as his headwaiter for special events. General Burns immediately started calling me Ritchie. Of all the previous generals, who were all great supporters of air power development, I found General Burns to be the greatest. He was able to combine the need for increased spending for air weapons while at the same pushing for better living conditions for the enlisted families. On one visit, General Burns took a few dignitaries on a tour of the housing in Niceville, Florida. Shortly afterward, family dwelling units were built on base in the Ben's Lake area.

When General Burns had visitors, I could be assured he was going to ask me to sing for them. He ordered the club officer to purchase several of his favorite songs, and whenever he requested "Ritchie to sing," I would sing his request. I sang with the Air Force Dance Band, Benny Goodman, Tommy Dorsey, and several other big-time bands. On one occasion, General Burns was invited to attend a farewell party for one of his officers who was being transferred. When he arrived and found me working the party, he asked me to sing for him. He introduced me to the friends he had brought with him – a trio that the private party had hired. I went over to the leader and asked if I could sing a number with them. I told them the name of the song General Burns had requested, but they refused. I tried to avoid General Burns, but he found me and asked when I would be singing. I made an excuse which he was not buying. I went back to the leader of the trio and explained the situation, and they still refused. I went back and told General Burns that they did not have the music and were unable to play for me. General Burns called the club officer over and instructed him to fire that band on the spot. It was embarrassing, but the general wanted his friends to hear me sing and I finally sang "Danny Boy" without music. Jim Crow lost that round.

On another occasion, General Burns requested that I sing with the band and this time they were able to back me up really well. After the performance, a colonel came to me and asked if we could talk for a moment. When we got together, he made me an offer. If I would be willing to leave the Air Force and work hard for two years, I would make the top of the music charts. I said that I would have to think about it. He gave me his address and said for me to think it over.

A frequent visitor was Congressman Bob Sikes, a member of the Armed Services Subcommittee, who knew me personally. In later years he would give Wayne Patrick a Congressional Appointment recommendation for West Point Military Academy.

Lieutenant Smith who lived next door was a great organizer. A graduate from Tuskegee, he organized a voter registration group. Our group began to transport people in the Fort Walton community to register to vote. Somehow the base got word of this and, within 30 days, we all had orders shipping us out of the area. Before I received my orders, Lillie Louise was born in mid March of 1958. Again, I had prayed to God to allot me a greater portion of love because my responsibility was increasing. This He did and I could not love anyone any more than I loved Lillie and still do. It was very hard leaving our friends and neighbors in North Hill gardens, the name of our subdivision.

In the process of clearing the base, I was walking from one office to the next when an automobile pulled up beside me. The man who had called me a black S.O.B stopped and asked if I needed a ride. He had his son as a passenger and he ordered him out of the front seat to make room for me. As his son was moving to the rear seat he said to him, "You will never be the man this one is." I immediately flashed back to the day I had prayed that I would prove to him that I was no S.O.B. Thereafter, each time I returned to the Eglin Engine Shop, he would greet me and inquire about my family.

I had accomplished two goals I set out to achieve. I had earned my seven-level and was promoted to technical sergeant within the time frame I had established.

Air Force air weapon systems were changing. Propeller-driven aircraft were being replaced. The new inventory was jet aircraft with supersonic speed. I knew I had to retrain into the new propulsion age. Pratt & Whitney had assigned two technical representatives to Eglin to train engine mechanics how to manage these new jet engines. I knew this was what I needed. I applied to cross train from reciprocating engines to jet engines. My request was granted. This meant starting from the beginning. Mr. Phil McGown accepted me into his jet propulsion class. I studied along with those white mechanics selected to become jet engine mechanics. Mr. McGown was a great instructor. He and Mr. Chipley taught the course. They taught the various systems and the quick engine change kits. Three months after the introductory training, I was upgraded to a five-level jet engine mechanic while I still maintained my position as an aircraft inspector. Phil McGown and I became very good friends. He was a Catholic that I would see whenever

I attended Mass at St. Mary's Catholic Church. He introduced me to Dorothy, his wife.

Before my rotation to my new assignment in Japan, I had earned my seven level in jet engines. The F-100, F-101 and F-102 were jet aircraft equipped with the PW J57 engines. I had learned the J57 engine to such an extent that I became an on-the-job trainer. Mr. Green, a black mechanic working the Engine Shop, was allowed by Mr. McGown to attend his classes. When Mr. Green completed the course, Mr. McGown gave him a Certificate and later told me that Mr. Green was so proud of that Certificate because he had never completed high school and it had a place of honor in his home.

At the time I received orders assigning me to Itazuke Air Base, Japan, General Burns was promoted to Lieutenant General and assigned Commander of 5th Air Force Japan. When he learned I was going to Japan, he started making arrangements for me to be on his staff in Tokyo.

The seven-year assignment at Eglin Air Force Base was over. I had arrived with three stripes and was leaving with five. The racial situation I had encountered had taken a very positive turn. I found great joy in knowing that my contribution had played a vital part in bringing about the change.

In retrospect, the following achievements were made over those seven years:

Started as a sergeant in 1951. Only had experience on one type of aircraft engine, the R-1820 installed on the B-17 aircraft

Learned to repair the R-1820 and R-1830 installed on C-47 aircraft

Learned to repair the R-2800 engine installed on B-26 aircraft

Learned to repair the J79 engine installed on F-104 aircraft

Became part time head waiter at the officer's club

Introduced to all eight of the four-star generals in the Air Force

Became acquainted with Congressman Bob Sikes

Promoted to staff sergeant

Married Helen May 20, 1953

Became a dad January 1954

Purchased our first home February 1955

Promoted to technical sergeant December 1955

Became a dad again December 1955
Completed jet engine training 1956
Became a Catholic June 2, 1957
Became a dad again March 1958
Those who impressed me most during this assignment:
    Mr. Jimmie Pierce, civilian manager of the Engine Shop
    Mr. Vern Cunningham, my first crew chief
    Mr. Holloway, foreman, aircraft repair
    Mr. Nadicksbernd
    Mr. Herman Brandley
    Captain Dean
    Chief Warrant Officer McDowell who signed my leave for Helen
and I to get married
    Mr. Bakersmith, sheet metal shop chief
    Mr. Frank Caruso, first to welcome me into the St. Mary's Catholic
community after my conversion
    Mr. Joe Barranco who taught me how to pray the rosary
    Monsignor Cunningham, pastor of St. Mary's Catholic Church
    General Norstad
    General Timberlake
    General Burns
    Master Sergeant Roberts
    Mr. Phil McGown, Pratt & Whitney Technical Representative
    Mr. Chipley, Pratt & Whitney Technical Representative

I learned as the years passed that there were many doors that were ajar. Yet, the spirit of Mrs. Lillie James, my elementary school teacher, was coaching me to remain prepared with my bags packed to enter whenever the door of opportunity opened. I found myself reflecting less upon those negative words "**most likely NOT to succeed or that boy won't amount to much.**" My future would still require those strong pillars of **faith, love and hope**, with me keeping them bound together with the thread of self-imposed spirituality. As I shared my talents with others, the achievements became even less challenging. It is so true that the more you give the more you receive. The depression baby was going up. **"How great thy art."** I turned to prayer and thanked my real father, God, for clearing the path for this little boy off of Jackson Street. The next assignment held its own opportunities.

The Rising Son in the Land
of the Rising Sun

In August 1958, the move began from Fort Walton Beach, Florida en route to Itazuke Air Base, Japan. The first stop was Indianapolis, Indiana. Mom traveled with us to spend time with Rebecca who had married Mack Montgomery and had moved there from Pensacola.

We spent two days visiting with them and resumed our travel to Travis Air Force Base, California.

Our 1950 Oldsmobile was loaded with Rickey, Pat and Lillie, traveling in her car bed. The little one took the trip in the car really well. We chose to travel the northern route because it was cooler. After a full day's travel, we were in Osceola, Iowa. At dusk, I started looking for a colored community to rest for the night. The children were tired, and I was unable to locate one. I prayed silently and suddenly it came to me. I had just converted to Catholicism, and I would find out if I could get help if I found a Catholic church. When I finally found one, I drove up to the rectory, got out nervously and rang the doorbell and a priest came to the door. I introduced myself and asked if he could recommend a place for my family to rest for the night. He thought for a moment and said, "I have a Catholic who owns a motel. I'm going to find out what kind of Christian she is." Father spoke loudly as I stood outside of the door. He placed a call and responded, "Yes it is a colored sergeant and his family." He answered, "Sure I know where you are located. I will direct them over there." The priest's name was Father Dere.

When we arrived at the motel, the female owner met us and showed us to our room. This was entirely new to me. To think of the situation I was in: it had never occurred to me, prior to this night, that I, a technical sergeant in the United States Air Force, traveling cross-country with my family, carrying out my orders in service of my country and, because of my colored race, would be unable to find resting quarters. Helen prepared the children for bed.

The next morning as we were leaving, the owner was very kind to us, and she invited us to come back if we ever came through again. It was breakfast time, and I was not sure where I would find food for the family. When I came to a restaurant, I looked for a side door for colored people but didn't see one. I left the family in the car and made an entry into the front door without opposition. The waitress came and gave me a menu and offered to take my order. I ordered pancakes for my whole family. The waitress wanted to know where my family was. I said they were in the car outside. She said, "Bring them in and sit down and enjoy your breakfast." As Helen was settling in and trying to balance Lillie on her lap, the waitress came over and offered to hold Lillie while Helen ate. This was all a new experience for me. Never before had I entered an all-white restaurant unchallenged and was able to sit and eat with other customers. I could see the fingerprint of God in all these developments. Mom had taught me that **The Lord is my shepherd, I shall not want**. She was right! Before we departed Indianapolis, Mom prayed, and I was aware that her prayers would remain with us.

The next day we traveled to Sidney, Nebraska. Once again, I looked for a colored community and again, I was unable to find one. This time we arrived at a Catholic church as the nuns were finishing their evening devotion. I approached the convent and one of the nuns greeted me. I told her the same story I had told to Father Dere: We were traveling and needed a place to rest for the evening. The other nuns came over and began playing with Rickey and Pat. One took Lillie and held her. A call was made to a motel and again we were welcomed. Helen asked one of the sisters where the colored community was located. The nun replied that there was no black community in the area. She explained that they had had one colored lady living with them for over a month, and she had really enjoyed herself. Helen performed her usual routine of getting the children prepared for bed.

The following morning, I did not hesitate to enter a restaurant. We had our breakfast and headed for Salt Lake City, Utah. When we arrived, again, I found a Catholic church and the priest was able to get us a house. I shopped at a nearby store while Helen took care of the children, and when I returned, we cooked up a storm and had a great meal. I was getting more confidence as we traveled, relying upon God and His Church.

Late the following evening, we arrived in Reno, Nevada, but I was unable to find a Catholic church so Helen and I decided to continue traveling on into California. We never dreamed of having to cross Donna Path at night. It was scary. Helen held Lillie tightly in her arms as we traversed those mountains. When we arrived in Auburn, California at eleven at night, I drove up to the first motel, entered and requested a room. We settled in for the rest of the night. One might say that Helen, the kids, and I were really on a *Faith* journey. The Catholic Church had helped tremendously. It was Sunday when we started the last leg of our journey to Travis Air Force Base to connect with our flight to Japan. We attended mass and enjoyed the rest of the ride.

Monday and Tuesday I took care of shipping our car to Japan and waited for the announcement of our flight. The children enjoyed the trip. Six-month-old Lillie was too young to know what was going on.

On August, 15, 1958, we boarded Honolulu Air Lines to Tachikawa, Japan. The trip was uneventful. When we arrived, transportation was waiting. We were provided quarters. All was well until Lillie began crying. She wanted to be fed. I went to get her formula, but discovered I had left her soy milk in the bag on the bus we had taken to the hotel. I searched through the streets to find milk but was unable to find any. Early the next morning, the Japanese driver brought the bag to me. An officer I knew when stationed at Eglin offered us a C-130 ride down from Tokyo to Itazuke. The load master placed Lillie's car bed between the mail bags the crew was delivering to Itazuke. The trip was over. We had reservations in the guest quarters. Helen and the children were comfortable and I processed into the 8th Field Maintenance squadron. I was assigned to the Propulsion Branch because I had taken this assignment under my new career field as a jet engine mechanic at the five-level.

Master Sergeant Savage was the non-commissioned officer in charge (NCOIC) of the branch and Captain Winfield Scott was the Maintenance Officer. I was assigned to the engine build-up section. There was a backlog of repairable engines to be returned to the States for overhaul. I was assigned the task to get rid of them. Within three weeks the backlog was gone. Captain Scott was so impressed that he wrote me an outstanding evaluation.

Our first house was in a sushi bar, but the quarters were too small, so when a larger place was available we moved.

Helen was pregnant with our fourth child. Jean and Earnest Clayton, our neighbors in Fort Walton, had arrived at Itazuke. They, too, had been shipped out for participating in the voter registration effort. They moved in with us until their quarters became available.

Things were going really good at the Propulsion Branch. I felt right at home because the shop was repairing J57 engines for the F-100 aircraft. The things I had learned from Mr. McGown proved very successful. Since I had gone through every phase of maintenance at Eglin, I was selected to instruct other mechanics on the repair procedure for the engine.

All was going well. Rickey was enrolled in kindergarten with Sister Maria who taught on base. Becoming close friends with Sister, we would have her visit our home regularly.

I joined the Holy Name Society. We met each second Sunday, attended Mass followed by a breakfast meeting. This was my first membership in an integrated organization. I was uncomfortable at the beginning but, as months went by, I became more involved and was elected vice-president.

In January 1959, General Burns, now Commander of the 5th Air Force under which the 8th Fighter Wing fell, came to Itazuke on his first visit. Colonel Montgomery brought him to the Propulsion Branch as one of the sections he liked. As the party made its way through the shop, General Burns caught sight of me. He interrupted his tour and came over and shook my hand, after which I gave him a very polite salute. He wanted to know about my family, and I said they were fine and settling in for a good tour of duty. General Burns said that Mrs. Burns was down at Base Operations and she would enjoy a visit from me. Colonel Montgomery offered his car, and I went to see her.

She thanked me for the musical album of their favorable songs I had recorded and given to them before we departed from Eglin Air Force Base. After General Burn's visit I gained friends that I never knew I had before after word got out that I was a personal friend of the General.

Helen was dealing with the move and pregnancy like the pro she was. I was progressing very well in my job. Ricky, Pat and Lillie were adjusting to their new environment. Helen volunteered to teach religious education and, at the end of the year, they had an appreciation dinner in one of the downtown restaurants. Helen asked me to sing for the group and, of course, I did. The priest asked if I would become cantor for the Mass and I accepted. Each week on Saturday, I rehearsed with a Japanese gentleman, and on Sunday I would lead the congregation in four hymns. It was there that I began my singing career in the Catholic Church

On a Saturday in March 1958, I received a call from the Red Cross that Mom had suffered a terminally cerebral hemorrhage and my presence was requested. I went to the priest and told him about the situation, and we prayed for Mom. Before I departed, I placed a call to General Burns and told him about the situation. He offered his help. This was a trying time for Helen because she loved Mom and was having a hard time accepting the news. We had never been apart for any length of time and here I was about to leave her overseas with three kids and one on the way.

After I departed, Sister Maria came over for a visit and found Helen upset. She returned to her convent and together her cloistered sisters prayed for Mom. Only a short time before my emergency, two Army soldiers stationed in Tokyo had been notified that they had deaths in their families and had come to Tachikawa to get a space-available flight back home. A lieutenant colonel bumped those soldiers from the flight in order to make room for his family to travel to Hawaii on vacation. One of the soldiers placed a call to 5th Air Force and insisted on speaking with General Burns. When he was able to get General Burns, he explained his situation. This really disturbed the general and he ordered the aircraft to return and off load the colonel's family and let those soldiers get home. The first reaction to General Burns call was that the Military Transport Command was not under his jurisdiction. General Burns' reply was if that aircraft was not returned, he would dispatch fighters to escort it back. The soldiers were boarded and were able to return home. The colonel was reprimanded. When I placed my call, not knowing what had taken place only a few days earlier, General Burns said, "Richie if you have any problems getting a flight, please give me a call."

A C-47 on a training mission came to Itazuke and gave me a ride to Johnson Air Base where I had attended school back in 1950. The officer of the day met me with a driver and got me to Tachikawa. When I arrived at the passenger terminal there was an announcement that Technical Sergeant Richardson had arrived. The way had been cleared as a result of the previous incident with the two soldiers going home to bury their loved ones.

When I arrived in Pensacola, Florida, it was noon. The Dubois' met me at the airport and took me directly to Baptist Hospital. I spoke with the nurses, and they said mom would most likely not be conscious of my presence. One told me the doctor had instructed them not go give her any medication because it was only a matter of time before she would pass away. I went to her bedside and spoke but had no response. After a moment I reached into my pocket and pulled out my rosary. I remembered how Mom had prayed for me when I was so sick and no one had expected me to make it through the night. Now I would pray for God's help because I was not prepared to lose Mom. It was noon and I prayed the rosary asking our Blessed Mother to intercede for me. I left under the same circumstances as Mom had when she had left me at Sacred Heart Hospital. Following that visit, I would go and be with her at noon, and I would pray the rosary. After four days she began to recognize me and she was so happy I was there. I told her I was praying the rosary each day to our Blessed Mother that she would intercede for us and ask her Son to share her life. Mom started praying the rosary with me each day at noon and one of the patients in the bed near her joined in with us.

After 14 days, Mom was discharged from the hospital not paralyzed nor did she suffer a loss of memory. Mom went on to live 22 years after that grave illness. She outlived the doctor who gave up on her recovery. *I was aware of our Blessed Mother's intercession.* Mom, a Methodist, prayed the rosary daily thereafter. I believe she was one of few, if any, Protestants who had the rosary prayed during her wake service.

During her illness I was able to arrange for her retirement from Civil Service. Rebecca was home and looked after her when I returned to Japan. Dorothy and her family were stationed in France.

When I returned to Itazuke, after being away for over 20 days, I found Helen and the children sick. In fact, a Red Cross message had been sent home for me to return to Itazuke to take care of her and the children. When I arrived, I took Helen and Lillie to the hospital. Helen was over seven months pregnant, and Lillie had double pneumonia. One doctor was going to discharge her and wanted to see her the next day. I waited because I was not sure Lillie would make it to the next morning. A member of the Holy Name Society was on the hospital staff, and he came over to welcome me home so I explained that Lille really needed help. He arranged for another doctor to see her. When they took her temperature, she was admitted immediately. Her fever was so high they had to bathe her in ice water. Helen was unable to go with me to the hospital with Lillie because she was extremely sick. The doctor that admitted Lillie also admitted Helen. Prayers were offered for the family, and I could see marked improvement in their health. The Japanese maid helped tremendously. I was granted additional leave until the situation at home was under control.

In late May of 1959, Carmen was born. Now I had four children for which to provide fatherly love. I prayed for grace to do just that. My work was going really well. I was still leading the singing at the Masses. I formed a drill team and performed at the six-man football games. General Burns kept in touch. He was so happy to learn that Mom had recovered from her illness and was doing well. Ten months after Carmen was born in early April 1960, Henri came along. Now we had five children. It was not over. In early June, the following year, Donna was born.

For additional entertainment a group formed the ITP Itazuke Performing Society. Once a month we entertained at the Non-commissioned Officer's Club. At the end of the Base Commander's tour, the group performed a farewell show for the colonel and his family. Three years were coming to an end. Our tour was almost over. During those three years, I added to my list of becoming the first colored to be elected President of the Itazuke Chapter of Toastmasters International, Vice-President of the Holy Name Society, organized a drill team, and to be selected as "Outstanding Supervisor of the month" for the field maintenance squadron. We had made new friends. Joining our list were: Jean and Chuck Farrington, Marge and Al Horton, Cool Momma White, and the Fearson's.

Our Japanese maids – Misawa and Mongi – really made life enjoyable. Misawa was with us when Carmen was born. Since Carmen was very fair and had red hair, Misawa was under the impression that all colored babies were born white and, as they grew older, the color came into their skin. She thought that Carmen was the most beautiful baby she had ever seen. She took it upon herself to invite our Japanese neighbors over to see her.

It was a miracle story about getting Mongi to work for us. She had retired, but was asked to keep the children when Bishop Fukahori confirmed me. When I took Mongi home after the ceremony, her husband was greatly surprised. Some months earlier I had run into him with my Oldsmobile. I had attended a briefing that clearly informed us if we had an accident involving a Japanese to report it at once. When this accident occurred, the gentleman was getting up and I pleaded with him to stay in place until the police came. He insisted that he was fine and that it was his fault. The interpreter told me that he wanted to forget it. I insisted that he wait for the police and that I wanted to pay for whatever happened. The interpreter said he would not take any money from you because it was his fault. I demanded that he take a certain amount of money that I had. He reluctantly took it and went away. A few weeks later, this gentleman came to my house carrying a basket of fruit. He had a letter written by a friend who knew English. I was afraid to open the letter because I knew this should have been settled by the police. When I read it, he had explained that he was a Christian. He was pleased with the kindness I had shown him. He spoke about me at his church services. He wanted me to have the fruit as a gift. He mentioned the following day he did have a few pains and he used the money for a doctor's visit and to get some repairs done to his bicycle. That night when I returned Mongi home, I discovered it was her husband. She came out of retirement to work for us until we rotated.

The return trip from Japan to the United States was uneventful.

Tour of Duty at Dover, Delaware

Lead Me, Guide Me, Lord!

The train ride from California to Florida was not as I had planned it. Helen had insisted on making the trip a short one by getting airline tickets for the family. After selling my point, we boarded the train from Los Angeles to New Orleans. On our first visit to the diner, I realized that I couldn't afford many meals there. When we arrived in El Paso, Texas, I got off the train and went to a nearby store. I purchased bread, milk, peanut butter, jelly, along with Franco-American spaghetti, which we all enjoyed during the rest of the trip. I had shipped my car from Japan in time for us to make connections in New Orleans. Sadly, something had happened and the car had not yet arrived. Consequently, we finished the trip to Pensacola on the train. Helen was right again.

When the proud grandparents met us, they were overwhelmed. We had left with three children and were now returning with six. The visit was good. Mrs. Waters, Helen's godmother, asked for all the other children. I checked on Mom's health and she was still doing fine. After three weeks at home, we resumed our travel to Dover, Delaware. We were now traveling with six kids and the same 1950 Oldsmobile. I rented a U-Haul for our luggage and other items to free up room in the car. Faced with the same discrimination problem we had in 1958 traveling to California, we stayed the first night at a motel in Atlanta, Georgia. The next evening we were in Charlotte, North Carolina. We found a colored motel – The Pines – right on Highway 29. On the following night we were in Richmond, Virginia, where Helen had a relative living there who generously took us in. On Saturday evening, we arrived in Dover, Delaware, tired and bedraggled. The on Base guest house was full, but we found a colored motel and spent the night. Next morning, I took the kids to Mass and, after Mass, I went to Base Billing and was assigned visiting quarters.

The Floyd Robertson's, who were our neighbors in Japan, had arrived in Dover ahead of us and invited us for dinner. Theda and Floyd had two girls and our children got along famously. On Monday I processed in. We were not there very long before Helen announced that she was pregnant again. Billy was born September 1962. *"Thy will be done."*

Helen and I became very active in the Dover Catholic program. We both joined the choir, and I became soloist. It was at this chapel that I sang the Ave Maria for the very first time. The invisible wall of fear that derived from racial situations in Pensacola was shattered when I became friends with the Hearon family. Karen, their daughter was the first white girl who wanted to hold hands with me as we walked together to our children's choir rehearsal. Not knowing how to handle that uncomfortable ordeal, I approached her parents and I was told not to feel that way because Karen really loved me. It took time but it worked. I later became the godfather of her first child.

Dover Air Force Base had its prejudices. I was a ranking technical sergeant but was not assigned work that would facilitate promotion. I worked the swing shift repairing Gas Turbine Units (GTUs) installed on the C-133 aircraft. This unit allowed the aircraft engines to be started without auxiliary power units. To some, this task was a very insignificant and minor maintenance effort, but I viewed it quite differently. Since the C-133 was the largest cargo aircraft in the Air Force, it was in great demand. Only a limited amount of these aircraft were purchased. Built like a banana, it was equipped with four T34-P-34 turbo propeller engines. The propulsion system was very complicated, and I saw this as an opportunity to excel.

In less than a year, I was assigned as supervisor of the evening shift, flight line repair section. With a crew of seven, we repaired GTUs and removed and replaced engines as needed. My reputation was growing as a troubleshooter. However, in spite of all the long hours I was working and the compliments received for supporting the C-133 aircraft, I still could not get promoted. When I questioned why I was not being considered for promotion, the answer always was, "You need more education." I needed to attend the NCO Academy they advised, and this I did. Then they said I needed more college courses. I enrolled at the University of Delaware and completed the courses; I was told that would help me get promoted. I took a position in the Propulsion Branch Office as an administrator. This would be a sure-fire way to get promoted. IT NEVER HAPPENED! Finally, I was told to get assigned to the jet engine test cell, one that no other black NCO had ever held, and it would surely get me promoted. Yahoo! I got the assignment.

While I was away attending an aircraft investigation course, Helen took it upon herself to gather all the information she could about my efforts to get promoted, compiled a package and sent it to President Lyndon B. Johnson.

One Friday afternoon, I received a call from Helen, and she was so excited. She said that the President had answered her letter. I asked her what letter and she said the one she had written asking why I could not be promoted. The President had said that I would get full consideration the next time the promotion board met. I was aghast. "Helen, you didn't?" She hung up on me.

I rushed home after work and questioned Helen on why she would do such a thing? She said, "Walter, please give me the keys to the Volkswagen." She was late for a Sodality meeting. She left. I immediately called Father Earley, our neighbor. The rectory was just across the street from our quarters. I went over, and I told him what Helen had done. He said that Helen had no chain-of-command. "She can write whomever she wants." He continued, "I am proud of her. I have wondered, too, why you were never promoted." I left and now I would have to let my Squadron Commander know what had happened. He answered the phone and said he was aware of the inquiry and wished his wife was that energetic. "Perhaps," he said' "I could get promoted."

Now the storm had blown over and Helen returned from church. The children had been bathed and all were in their beds. She asked, "Now what do you want to talk with me about?" I said, "Nothing." President Johnson was right; in May 1963, I became the first African-American technical sergeant to be promoted to master sergeant in the Field Maintenance Squadron in Dover, Delaware. The Squadron Commander called Helen before he called me to let her know that I was promoted. From that time on, President Johnson became a friend of our family. I personally met him during his campaign for election. *Lead me; guide me Lord!* Or at least, guide Helen.

Unfortunately, a very serious mysterious problem persisted with the C-133 aircraft. Dover had experienced two fatal in-flight accidents. Many technicians and specialists had worked long hours trying to figure out how to correct this problem. I was supervisor of the test stand operating the T34 engine. I discussed this problem with our team and the outcome of our "what-if" drill was to experiment on engine oil temperatures. The main engine oil temperature was already incorporated in the telltale system. In the nose section where the propeller was installed, the same engine oil system lubricated the high-speed pinions located in the nose case. The test stand crew found a capped-off plug in the nose case and suggested that a separate oil temperature bulb be placed there to record the difference between the oil temperature lubricating the main engine bearing and the temperature of oil lubricating the high speed pinions gear.

After installing the wiring to a gauge on the console, it was found that on a normal engine run the temperature spread was only 20 degrees. When we finally tested an engine where the temperature spread exceeded 20 degrees the engine was shut down, the main engine oil screen was removed and it was found to be loaded with metal filings. The engine was returned to the engine repair section and the nose case was removed and one of the high-speed pinions was failing. The friction caused the oil temperature to rise and the discolored metal in the nose case justified the rubbing prior to a failure. This simple temperature bulb costing less than $50.00 corrected a major problem. Afterwards, aircrews could monitor the temperature and shut down an engine with a 20-degree difference. There was never another C-133 aircraft lost due to airborne nose case failure. Simultaneously, I joined the Knights of Columbus and was president of the Dover Catholic Holy Name Society. Soon, I was invited to attend the Wilmington, Delaware Holy Name Society breakfast and our guest was Archbishop Sheen.

In mid July of 1966, Carl was born; the family was complete. I had been selected for an assignment in Southeast Asia, which had been deferred until Carl arrived. Weeks after his birth, I received orders assigning me to Pleiku, Vietnam.

Dover, Delaware was a great assignment. It gave me the opportunity to enter new doors for which I was prepared. I continued attending daily Mass, a practice I had started in 1959 while stationed in Japan. It was during lent when the Priest announced that instead of giving up smoking and beer and your family, why not try attending Mass more frequently during this holy season. That worked well for me. However Helen, who suffered with allergies – would have preferred that I stop smoking.

The Chief of Maintenance, Colonel Gunekurt, selected me as the number one troubleshooter for the propulsion system on the C-133 aircraft. It did not matter where a C-133 broke down, the colonel would seek my advice and the aircraft would make it home safely. At the end of my tour, the colonel recommended that I be promoted ahead of all the other eligible master sergeants to the grade of senior master sergeant.

Our work at the chapel brought us in contact with many outstanding priests such as: Fathers Gilchrist, William Campbell, Earley, Louis Schmidt, Jake Doonan, and Father Meade, who finally became a Two-Star General and Chief of Chaplains for the United States Air Force.

Rickey, Pat and Lillie received their first holy communion at Dover. Lillie's first communion was scheduled while I was competing at the command level for "Tops in Blue." I won and was to go worldwide but instead I gave my position to the runner-up to be back at home for Lillie's first reception of the sacrament.

Dover was the mortuary center for all remains returning from overseas to families east of the Mississippi. The procedure was to assign an escort of the same rank or higher who was practicing the same religious beliefs, to accompany remains back home to the families and to attend the funeral services. I was called upon frequently for this stressful job, yet it was consoling to meet the families and share some insight on the military. Most of the families had no knowledge of the military life and could engage in conversations that would give them answers to questions they had never asked.

I was requested to sing for a retiring schoolteacher at a banquet in downtown Dover. She wanted me to sing, *"How Great Thou Art."* I had to learn the song but afterwards it became one of my favorite hymns. The title of this book is proof.

At Dover I organized a drill team similar to the one I had done in Japan. We were invited to march in loyalty day parades in Delaware and New Jersey. The Squadron received many letters complimenting us for so proudly representing the Air Force.

In February of 1966, I received my Fourth Degree in the Knights of Columbus as a gift from Father William Campbell from the base chapel for all the services I had rendered. I was the only Black Knight receiving the degree.

Dover, Delaware provided us with the opportunity to meet the Stotts. They became our best friends. Dottie was not Catholic. When she learned that Helen was pregnant with Carl, she took instructions and was brought into the church in time to become Carl's godmother.

Daddy Dubois passed away while we were in Delaware. We drove down to attend the funeral while Helen was pregnant with Carl. We wanted Mother Dubois to come back to Delaware with us, but she refused. When Lillie was preparing to take her first Holy Communion, we invited Mother Dubois to come up and she agreed. She included a visit with her sister-in-law living in Richmond where we had stayed when traveling up to Dover. While she was there she purchased a song and brought it with her to Dover. She said that it was a perfect description of me and she had bought it for me. *"If I Can Help Somebody My Living Will Not Be in Vain."* That became the title of my second musical album.

The seven years at Dover Air Force Base were great for our family. With the children enrolled in the Catholic school, Helen and I used the same three-pillar concept in raising our children. Home represented *Love*. The church and religious activities represented *Faith*_and the school represented *Hope*. All of this was bound together with the strong thread of *Spirituality*.

These were difficult times. I worked three jobs to make ends meet. Helen helped by taking sewing jobs. She made most of the children's clothes. We bought vegetables from the Mormon farmers' market and canned most of them. The neighbors were kind and would pass on to us extra food items they had purchased on sale. I kept my credit union account maxed out. I made friends with the owner of the Western Auto store in Dover who allowed me credit to buy Christmas toys for the kids. I was told that I was eligible to get food stamps, but I never did pursue that suggestion. The family never missed Mass on Sundays and I tried to attend daily Mass as often as I could. God looked after us. We had a house, a Volkswagen minibus and food. With all these blessings, we were very happy. Rickey and Pat were altar servers. I was happy to sing Handel's *"Messiah"* with the Dover Catholic Choir. It brought back memories of my freshman year in college.

The civil right's movement was in full bloom. I was in New York on burial escort duty when Martin Luther King marched on Washington. The undertaker I had met during my first escort duty offered me his house to stay in while he joined a group and traveled to Washington to take part in the march.

As the chapter of this assignment was ending, *The Little Boy from Jackson Street* could reflect on the blessings of this era:

1. Promotion to master sergeant
2. Promotion to senior master sergeant
3. Helped open the door for other technical sergeants to be fairly considered for promotion to master sergeant
4. A leadership role in solving a critical problem with the C-133
5. Happy children
6. Fantastic friends
7. Strides in civil rights
8. A wonderful wife who could move presidents to action

Hey Papa: *"How Great Thou Art"*

The Agonies of Vietnam
(Then Back to Dover Air Force Base)

Have Thine Own Way, Lord

For a very short period in my life, I found myself in a pervasive, fearful mode. When I was notified that I was being assigned to Vietnam, fear sprouted in my mind. Thoughts of whether or not I would become a casualty and the responsibilities I would leave behind were inescapable. Just the thought of leaving Helen to raise eight children without me fueled these thoughts and created fear.

After my arrival in Saigon my thoughts were still causing a great deal of consternation. I realized that my faith, built over the years, had been engaging in a war with fear. For years I had lived securely under the blanket of freedom. Even though it contained prejudices and discrimination, I had never had this level of anxiety to deal with.

After I attended Mass one Sunday morning, I found some consolation, which lasted only for a short time. Following lunch at the NCO club, which was located near the building used for the mortuary, I sat outside and watched a parade of helicopters bringing in bodies of soldiers who had made the ultimate sacrifice. Again my apprehension soared.

I felt mentally and spiritually paralyzed, which made it hard to concentrate on a fitting prayer which might calm the fright and restore the faith I had developed over the years. It was hard for me to imagine God being there in the midst of all this fighting and killing. I found it hard to pray the rosary and to let my mind focus on the mysteries. I kept thinking of the countless times I had prayed the sorrowful mysteries and felt the sorrow in my heart that Our Lord had suffered for our salvation, but that Sunday I was unable to meditate while watching the frequency of the helicopters bringing remains from the heavy combat activity going on north of Saigon. The three pillars upon which I had built my faith were under extreme pressure. I discovered that fear, when allowed to grow, can eradicate faith or at least wound it severely. *Fear is a terrible state of mind.* I had experienced numerous situations, which had frightened me but nothing to compare with the hopelessness I was dealing with at this time.

Arriving in the central highlands, I realized that Pleiku would be my home away from home for the next 12 months. As I resumed attending daily Mass, I began to regain my faith and the terror began to fade away. Over time, the perpetual sound of artillery fire, bombs exploding, and late night rocket attacks, did not reignite the fear I had been experiencing. My faith in God was once again in control of my life . . . it was winning the war.

After 12 months of living and worshiping God in a war zone, I had survived. I had again resumed my faith journey and had received orders to return to Dover, Delaware.

After Mass one evening, I had a message waiting for me to meet the Squadron Commander at the Officer's club. When I arrived, he congratulated me for being promoted to the grade of Senior Master Sergeant, a promotion which followed my performance at Dover Air Force Base, Delaware.

On March 1967, the Base announced that a talent contest would be held to seek participants for the United States Air Force worldwide talent show named, "Tops in Blue". This was the talent show I had removed myself from a year earlier to be home with Lillie who was receiving her first holy communion. I entered and won in two categories. The team winning in Saigon was selected to go to Okinawa to participate in the Pacific Air Force Command finals. I won at both levels. General Westmoreland lifted the restrictions which prevented troops from leaving Vietnam to participate in other contests outside the war zone.

When I arrived at Okinawa, it was quite different from my first tour of duty in 1949. Dorothy and her family were stationed there. We spent three wonderful days together. She attended the talent contest and was thrilled when I won and would be going forward to the United States to participate in the world-wide contest. Neither Dorothy nor I knew that this parting would be the last time we would see each other alive. She died in St. Louis, Missouri (where her husband Calvin, and sons Calvin and Brian, were stationed), after suffering a massive stroke on her 39th birthday. It was during the funeral services that the choir sang "May the Work I've Done Speak for Me", a song that has stayed with me through the years.

I arrived back at home exactly three months after I had departed for Vietnam. It was great timing for Helen. We had purchased a new home in Fort Walton Beach before I departed and there were things I needed to take care of which I was able to handle during that very short stay. I competed in the world-wide contest but lost intentionally. Had I won, it would have meant traveling with the show and returning to Vietnam later for another full tour of duty.

Shortly after leaving Vietnam, the Tet Offensive exploded. Intense fighting took place in the central highlands where I had just left. News from the base was favorable. Again, the Air Force did not suffer any losses. Fleetingly, a flash of fear once again entered my mind, but I could only think gratefully of all the places I had traveled while stationed in Vietnam and never fired upon. My faith took control and the Holy Spirit within me inspired me to thank God, my true Father, for protecting me over the year. During the last rocket attack I experienced while inside a bunker, a chief master sergeant I had worked with approached me and said that he had observed my behavior over the past year and was impressed with the manner in which I conducted myself when associating with others. He said, "You must have a wonderful family." I said I surely did. He continued by saying how he had noticed my conduct while associating with the Vietnamese women, and never once could he or anyone else knowing me accuse me of being unfaithful to my marriage. Those were inspiring comments following the final rocket attack before my departure. I admit that I prayed daily for that Vietnamese who fired on us for a complete year without hitting a barrack, aircraft, or an airman. My prayer was that he would not be replaced with someone more accurate. I consider my conduct, which heavily included my strong faith in God and commitment to serve contributed to the award of the Bronze Star medal I was given for service above and beyond the call of duty. I never passed up the opportunity to praise **HIM** during my tour in Vietnam. *"Have thine own way, Lord."*

Someday, history will reveal the indisputable fact that President Johnson was instrumental in restoring freedom and justice in Vietnam, a country which had endured civil war for many years. As I look back, even in spite of my fears, I am grateful that I had the opportunity to spend time providing entertainment for our troops to help reduce the fear and tension they were experiencing.

The Vietnam tour aided tremendously in strengthening our family ties. While there, I learned that the family formed the "Be Good to Mother Club". Each week, we exchanged voice recordings. The children shared their stories and I would respond. Carl was much too young to participate; however, the tape recorder used to facilitate our meetings was kept in the front hall closet. So, when anyone would ask Carl where his dad was, he would point to the closet . . . a heart-rending memory.

On return, I spent three weeks home with the family. Helen had delayed Christmas until I got back. The Christmas tree was decorated and most of the presents were still under it. The children had worked up a Christmas play, and I was their audience. Things were well organized, and I was really enjoying the performance until Carl – now over a year old – had a hard time getting Brutus, the family dog, to act like a sheep. When Lillie, the genesis and director of the Christmas play, tried to get Carl to participate, he replied, "Brutus is not a sheep, he is a dog." Beyond the incident with Carl and the dog, everything went well. We opened gifts and, together again had our delayed Christmas dinner.

This was my first visit in our new home. Helen and the family had moved in while I was in Vietnam. I enjoyed the comfort and complimented Helen for designing it as she had. My return to Dover was uneventful. My first stop was the Base Chapel. Father Meade was still there as well as Father Donaan. Both priests welcomed me and immediately asked me to rejoin their ministry. I did.

Colonel Mary Wallace, Chief Nurse of the Hospital, was still there. It was her mother who had befriended me before I left for Vietnam.

Mrs. Wallace wrote me faithfully. She had sent me "*The Christmas Guest*," a poem I read to the troops in Vietnam and one I have recited every year since 1967.

Much to my regret the prejudices that I encountered when I had first arrived at Dover in 1961 still existed. Black Airmen were being discharged for "failure to comply." This was a regulation used to discharge black airmen who were considered to have a bad attitude. I was a senior master sergeant assigned to the midnight shift. Mr. Wiggins, the Engine Shop Foreman, was very familiar with my professional knowledge pertaining to the C-133 aircraft and knew that I could handle the heavy workload with which they had tasked me. I was greatly disturbed with the way the young black airmen were being treated. I made my concerns known to the first sergeant whose reply was that I had nothing to do with this. I replied that I did have something to do with it, and I wanted to know how they had concluded that these black airmen were failing to comply. His reply was, "Have you looked closely at these black airmen?" I stated that I had and I found nothing wrong with them. I asked, "What was his problem?" He said that they were refusing, when told by their supervisors, to get a haircut. This was the period when the AFRO hairstyle was the "thing" for black people. The black airmen who wanted to let their hair grow were considered as "failing to comply" and were discharged under less than honorable conditions. (A general discharge makes it very difficult for one to obtain a security clearance required by most defense contracts.) It was after I visited the base OSI and told them what was going on that this practice stopped. Afterwards, the Air Force reviewed its uniform and hairstyle policy which was amended to permit black airmen to let their hair grow. The white airmen benefited as well: they were allowed to wear side burns.

The Stotts family was still in Dover. John likewise had been requested to return to Dover AFB after his tour in Vietnam because of his extensive knowledge of the C-133 aircraft. Unfortunately, the senior master sergeants who had arrived at Dover and assigned to the engine shop while I was in Vietnam had little knowledge in troubleshooting the C-133 aircraft. I straightened out a lot of their uncompleted work by having my crew come on duty after hours.

The C-141 was the aircraft selected to replace the retiring C-124 and C-133. I was requested back to Dover to help phase out the C-133.

Dover received its first C-141 which was tagged by Military Air Command to be the "Lead the Fleet" model. This required fully utilizing the aircraft to fly as many hours as possible during a 24-hour period. Whenever the C-141 would land, another aircrew would be waiting to take off again.

While returning to Dover from a trip to Europe, the aircrew radioed ahead that one of the engines was due time change. The maintenance officer notified me and I briefed my maintenance team that we would have only five hours to remove and replace an engine on the "Lead the Fleet" aircraft when it arrived. My team prepared the location where the work would be done with the maintenance stands and the replacement engine standing by. After the aircrew had taxied the aircraft into position and the engines were shut down, the clock started. This period allowed the new crew time to make flight plans and arrange whatever mission they were going to fly. From the time the engine was shut down until the time I personally signed off the completed work, we had used up exactly *three hours*. This would become the standard that the Military Airlift Command would use. The maintenance officer was so pleased, he wrote letters of commendation for the men and I later made recommendations for each airman involved to receive the Air Force Commendation medal which they did receive.

While at Dover unaccompanied, I got involved with the youth development group in that city. Together, we were able to perform a musical show in one of three local high schools that drew very favorable reviews from the community at large.

The priest operating a boys' school in Clayton, Delaware asked me to work with the boys and help them form a drill team. Our team performed in several parades. My singing voice was gaining recognition, and I was also involved with the choirs. Our performances were well received. The priest asked if I had ever considered recording my singing voice? I had not. He asked for a demo tape, explaining that he had a friend who wanted to hear me sing. I recorded a demo and gave it to father. A few weeks later, I got a call to come to New York for an interview with M.M. recording studio.

A Mr. Lewis interviewed me and offered a contract, but I had to refuse. He asked me why and I explained that I had only 19 years in service, and I wanted to stay for 20, that I was a senior master sergeant and wanted to make chief. He understood and promised he would keep the contract open until I would make up my mind. God had other plans.

"Have Thine Own Way Lord" became the hymn I sang mostly as I drove alone to various places to which I was invited. The year was moving on. Helen and the kids came to Dover during school vacation to visit with me. While they were there, we took a trip to New York to visit Mrs. Smith who had asked that I stay in touch with her after her son had been killed in an auto accident in Germany. Mother Smith lived in a beautiful condominium overlooking the old polo grounds where the New York Giants once played baseball. Mother Smith had arranged for some of her friends to come over and meet Helen and the kids. I had heard the kids sing after my return from Vietnam, and I asked if they would sing for Mother Smith. They did and after they finished, the visitors took up a collection and gave it to them.

My reputation was gradually gaining recognition from General Wallace, our Wing Commander. The remarkable turn around task on the "Lead the Fleet" aircraft had reached his office. It was the beginning of the year, and *"Operation Reforger"* was being planned. I was selected to go to Lages in the Azores to take care of engine problems as the C-133 used that base as a crew rest en route to Germany.

It was not long after I arrived that a C-133 aircrew called ahead and said they would need an engine change. I had one airman assigned on this TDY with me. When the aircraft arrived, I arranged for it to be placed in the maintenance hangar. The engine shop had a spare engine on hand. After we removed the old engine, we began configuring it for the slot from which the old engine had been removed. The crew rest was 24 hours. The two of us worked sixteen hours until the new engine was installed and operationally checked. The aircrew was able to take off on time. The Chief of Maintenance invited me to his office and asked if I would consider an assignment there and supervise his engine shop. I asked for time to think about it. The rest of the C-133 aircraft were ferried through Lages without delay. I asked the Chief of Maintenance to allow me time to discuss his offer with my family but when I returned to Dover, I was selected again to go TDY to assist with an operation going on with joint allied forces where the C-141 aircraft was to be introduced for the first time. I accepted and it was a very rewarding TDY.

I will always remember when the message came over the PA system that Lieutenant General Whip Wilson was flying the lead aircraft over to the exercise. I later had a chance to meet the General when he came to visit Dover AFB. To say he was an interesting General would be a gross understatement. When he announced his visit to the Base, he requested an audience with the young airmen but also wanted senior NCOs to be present. He would ask the young airmen to air their problems and he made it clear that if any one of those airmen would be rebuked for raising a complaint that he would personally take care of the situation. This really opened up the discussion. Those airmen complained about everything from working long hours to the living conditions in the barracks, the food and the list went on. The General would ask if there was any NCO present from the squadron where the airmen were experiencing these problems. I spoke up on one complaint about tools in our tool crib. I explained that the policy was established mostly for accountability and not to harass the troops. He wanted to know if the instructions were clear and, if not so, would I make sure that they were. I accepted the task. The instructions to the NCOs present were to go back and correct the problems. If the complaints were severe enough, the general was known to replace the Commander on the spot. There was always tremendous anxiety whenever General Wilson held those meetings. The out briefing would be with the Wing Commander. The instructions were: take care of the problems or he would personally check for the corrective action.

After a year in Vietnam, I spent this interesting year without my family. General Wallace received word that the Chief of Maintenance at Lages had requested that I be assigned there to supervise the Propulsion Branch, but he wanted to know if I really wanted the assignment. I said that I would prefer an assignment to the Philippines. I had told my family I would request such an assignment there because of the positive experiences I had had there during my visits while stationed in Vietnam. General Wallace said, "Well, if your choice is the Philippines, I will work to get you there." He explained, "I requested for you to return to Dover because we still had the C-133 aircraft and now that the C-141 is operational, we will start phasing out the C-133. He expressed his appreciation for all the work I had done to keep the aircraft flying safely.

Shortly afterward, I received orders assigning me to Clark Air Base, Philippine Islands. This time, leaving Dover was much less emotional than the previous one. John and Dottie Stotts had rotated to Bermuda while the Jackson's remained there. I was the godfather of two of their children. Father Meade had rotated to Thailand, and would later become the "Chief of Chaplains" of the Air Force.

When I reflect on this short tour at Dover, I think the crux of my work was not solely to retire the C-133 aircraft from service but to relieve those young black airmen from the penalty of general discharges for standing firm in their desire to live out their black heritage. I would view Dover from my rear view mirror, not returning there for the rest of my Air Force career. *Have Thine Own Way Lord.*

Pass Me Not O Gentle Saviour

Clark AB, Philippines

I spent my usual three weeks of leave at home before leaving for the Philippines. Mom was doing well. Dr. Hickson had accepted her as a patient after her first doctor had given up on her. He looked forward to her appointments just to get a good laugh "from the lady with a great sense of humor."

While on my way to Mass, I had my radio on and an announcement was made that the city needed help. I offered my aid and worked for two weeks on a garbage truck. It was quite a unique experience, one that gave me a first-hand perspective and appreciation for the people who do this difficult, grimy work every day.

After making arrangements for the family to travel in July, I departed for the Philippines, not knowing that the ensuing years would fortify the pillars of *faith, hope, and love . . . And at the same time amplifying my love for God and my brethren.*

Over time, I learned that before any worthy work is consummated for God, Satan attempts to disrupt the whole plan. On takeoff from Anchorage, the aircrew members experienced a problem. After reaching the required airspeed, they were unable to lift the aircraft off the runway.

During the three-hour wait for the radar system to be repaired, ice accumulated on the wings. The ground maintenance crew failed to defrost the wings and the aircraft had no lifting power. A similar situation had happened earlier and all 121 aboard had been killed. I felt that we were in trouble and uttered a silent prayer and, instantly, we lifted off the runway, but another threat was the mountain just ahead at the end of the runway. We eluded both problems. Thanks Dad.

My assignment as superintendent of the largest propulsion branch in the Pacific Air Force (PACAF) consisted of supplying engines for 13 locations in Southeast Asia. I was responsible for the build up and repair of J57 engines for the F-102; J79 for the F-4; R-1830 engines for the C-47, and T56 engines for the C-130 aircraft.

At the initial meeting with my section supervisors, I asked for their support and cooperation. I assured them I would be available to help them.

I had one major request and that was for them not to operationally test any engines on the test stand after dark. I explained it was a safety precaution because at night, with all of the artificial lights used; it is extremely difficult to distinguish if the fluid leaking from an engine is jet fuel or water.

One evening after dark, I got a call notifying me that one of my young airmen had been injured at the test stand. When I arrived, I asked the supervisor what had happened. He said the engine had experienced a compressor stall while operating at 100 percent. I knew this was not true. In my experience with operationally checking the J57 engines, there had never been a compressor stall without a cause. Normally, something would have to obstruct a large portion of the airflow into the engine to cause one. The supervisor had not told me the truth.

I learned, after talking with the injured airman, what had really happened. When he had stepped outside the test cell door to check for leaks, he had gotten too close to the intake screen and the suction from the compressor at 100 percent RPM drew him into the protection screen and when the compressor stall occurred, the force propelled him into the wall of the building some twenty feet away.

I then questioned the supervisor why they were testing the engine after dark and he said he wanted to complete the job. I reminded him of my policy and told him he was fired! He protested, "You cannot fire me because I'm the best test cell operator in the Pacific." I left the test stand and went to the hospital to visit the young airman. He was all shook up but not seriously injured. The following morning, I reported to the Chief of Maintenance what really had caused the accident. I told him that I had relieved the supervisor because he had not told the truth about what caused the compressor stall. He in turn explained it to the Wing Commander. It was only weeks after I changed supervisors at the engine test stand that we had all of the repairable engines on the ready line. It was the first time in years that the branch had had all repairable J57 engines serviceable.

Colonel McNeff, 405th Wing Commander, was pleased. He was concerned about the availability of spare J-57 engines and arranged a visit to the branch. What he saw impressed him. The colonel gave me one of the best Airman Performance Reports (APR) that I had ever received. I am sure it was helpful in my promotion to chief master sergeant that followed. Thanks Dad.

Helen and the kids arrived in July, 1969. To keep busy while waiting for them, I worked part-time at the Top Hat NCO club where I had brought my band from Vietnam. *Pass me not o gentle Saviour.*

One evening while I was having dinner at the Top Hat Club, a Filipino gentleman approached me and asked if I was Catholic and if I would like to attend a Cursillo – all in the same breath. Without thinking about it, I said yes.

When I got home from work I told Helen that I was going to a Cursillo. She wanted to know what a Cursillo was. I didn't know. I did know that the Filipinos held good parties with plenty of good food, so I was enthusiastic.

On Wednesday, two gentlemen came and drove me to Apalat, Pampango. I had no idea what was about to happen. For the next three days and nights, I encountered Jesus Christ during lectures and well-planned activities in a way that I had never dreamed of. I realized another level of *faith, hope, and love.* I rededicated my life to Jesus, prayed a lot, laughed and cried. This was truly a rebirth and a deeper love for Jesus. I really did not want the course to end. Although I wanted to share this experience with Helen, I was so elated that I found it hard to really explain it to her. I strongly recommended that she attend a Cursillo and experience the encounter with Jesus for herself. Initially she refused but later consented. After her three days, she too had a spiritual renewal in the spirit of love for God and others. Thanks Dad.

During the summer 1970, the Chief Master Sergeant Promotion list was released. On that day, I was at Mass when I received a call from my Commander to report to the orderly room immediately. When I arrived, the Commander accused me of being responsible for that serious accident which happened at the jet engine test cell months earlier. He had written a letter of reprimand for review before forwarding it to the Wing Commander. Initially, I refused to accept the letter. He gave me a direct order to open the letter. When I opened the envelope, a set of Chief Master Sergeant Stripes fell out. My anger had turned to joy in an instant. He congratulated me, as did the others while standing outside his office. Arriving back at the chapel, Helen wanted to know what was so important that I had to report to the Commander. I showed her the new stripes. I had reached the top rung of the enlisted military career ladder. I offered prayers during that Mass for all the Officers, Non-Commissioned Officers, Airmen, Civilians, and my family for all they had done to make that day possible. *Thanks Dad.*

In the seventies, Clark Air Base was going through a terrible period dealing with racial issues. The problem was at such a serious level that at any time a race riot could happen. Discontent within the enlisted ranks was explosive. Growing up with segregation had conditioned me on how to avoid such an environment.

At one of my formations, the black airmen appeared wearing black wristbands. I questioned why. I was told that the wristband was considered jewelry. From what I knew, the black wristbands were associated with the black power movement in the United States. I asked them to remove the wristbands and wear them with their civilian clothes. The following morning they appeared in my formation again wearing their black wristbands. I asked why. One black airman said, "We had a meeting with the Squadron commander and he told us that you had no right to tell us what we could not wear. I dismissed the formation, went to my office and wrote out my resignation and sent the letter to both the Squadron and the Wing Commanders and went home.

Before long, Captain Newton and Captain Pugh, both black fighter pilots of the 523rd, came to my home and requested that I come with them. The Wing Commander had sent for me. I initially refused to return until I had orders reassigning me to another organization. Both officers said they were not to return without me, so I went with them. The Wing Commander made it clear that I was his chief and if any airmen had a problem following my orders that he would take care of them. After the meeting, the Squadron Commander apologized. He said he realized he had made a terrible mistake. I said that I needed his support if I was to have discipline and maintain the fleet of F-4 aircraft I was in charge of. He committed to strongly support me.

Captain Fig Newton approached me and asked what could be done to ease the racial tension. I explained that he had to realize that, as an officer he had no choice. I continued that although he may have personal feelings about the situation, he was first an officer and that excluded him from any one race. We represented them all.

From our discussions, the impetus of a race relations committee was formed. Captain Newton, a very brilliant man, was facilitator during meetings between white and black airmen. Grievances were taken seriously. The black airmen wanted more soul music in the clubs and the white airmen wanted more country and western. Both got their requests. Tension was eased. As the committee continued to meet and commanders got involved, Clark Air Force Base became a model for other bases to manage their racial differences.

A suggestion sent to Lt/Gen. McNickle, Commander 13th Air Force, was the genesis for a soul show called the "Soul Twister," a production which did a great job mending relationships between white and black airmen. The boy from Jackson Street was instrumental in removing racial resentments that he had once faced. The Soul Twisters traveled extensively throughout Thailand, Vietnam, and Guam.

According to Air Force Times, "Master of Ceremonies Walt Richardson was wildly received as the group's second Bangkok show played for 2,000 excited Thai young people under sponsorship of the U.S. Information Service. Richardson drew a tremendous response with a pantomime of an American G.I. on his first date with a new girl."

"Emcee Chief Master Sergeant. Walt Richardson is well-known to base audiences as well as AF worldwide."

Becoming deeply involved with the Cursillo movement, I befriended a great number of Filipinos. Some of my brother Cursillistas held very high positions within the Filipino government. During my involvement in the Cursillo movement, I met Mr. Kit Lujumco, a retired musician who accompanied me during a number of the off-base singing engagements, mostly for Cursillos.

Because of a humanitarian act, I was selected as the "Most Outstanding Airman of the Year" for Pampango Province. The monsoon season was severe in 1972. Heavy rains for a long period of time caused flooding, and travel by automobile was impossible. Bridges were washed away. The roads between Angeles City and Manila were also washed away.

A taxi driver came to my office and said that he had Mr. Lujumco with him and that he needed medical attention. I escorted them to the hospital and went inside to get help. The administrative officer sent a doctor outside to learn what the problem was since I didn't know. When the doctor looked at his foot and saw the swelling, he knew that he needed emergency help. Mr. Lujumco, a diabetic, had punctured his foot and had gone over three weeks without any medical treatment because the roads to Manila were closed. He was admitted into the hospital under the *"Life or Limb Agreement"* between the two governments. Three hours later, the medical team had amputated the problem. Gangrene had set in and the foot had to be removed. A few days later they removed another portion of his leg. After two weeks recovering in the hospital, Kit was discharged. When the attendant went in to clean his room, they discovered in the table drawer near his bed, every pain pill that they had issued to him all wrapped up in a small napkin with a note saying that he had offered his pain and suffering to God and America for saving his life. That humanitarian act gained me the recognition of being selected as the Air Force Outstanding Airman of the Year.

Helen and I traveled to Hawaii, PACAF headquarters where General O'Keefe pinned on me the Outstanding Airman Ribbon. It never dawned on me what an honor it was to be selected as one of the twelve outstanding airman of the air force. After the aircraft had landed at Hickam Air Force Base, Hawaii, the Pilot announced that on board was one of the 12 outstanding airmen of the air force and to please remain seated until he and his spouse had deplaned. Helen and I were greeted by CMSGT Jackie Godwin, our escort who was a previous recipient of the outstanding airman award. I later learned that in that year, there had been fewer outstanding airmen ribbons awarded than Congressional Medals of Honor. The Command sponsored us as we attended numerous receptions and resided at the Royal Hawaiian "Pink" hotel in beautiful Waikiki Beach. ***How Great Thou Art!***

In Washington, we stayed at the famous Watergate Hotel. During the banquet honoring the outstanding airmen and our wives, Major General Chappie James (my first boss) came up to me and said, "Man, Mom would be proud of you," and I said in reply, "I am sure she is equally as proud of you." He and I had a good visit and it really struck home to me what a great honor it is to be one of the best in the Air Force when you sit at the head table and look at four-star generals seated on the lower level. Our stay in Washington included a visit to the White House, the Tomb of the Unknown Soldier, a television broadcast, and an off -Broadway show at the Kennedy Center featuring Ben Vereen in "Pippin."

During the final banquet honoring 25 years of the Air Force as a separate unit of the Department of Defense, Arthur Godfrey narrated the evening's activities. Members of the group were guests at a special banquet sponsored by General Ryan, the Chief of Staff of the Air Force who sat next to Helen during the official photo. As we talked at length, he said that he was retiring soon but before retirement, he was gong to make a final swing in the Pacific theater and that he would come by my propulsion branch.

During my visit at home, I experienced mixed feelings. "Papa Dear," my stepfather, had passed away, and I knew about it, but mom – knowing that I would be in the U.S. for the Outstanding Airman Award - suggested that I not come home for the funeral. Rickey was glad to see us. He was doing real well in junior college. What a proud moment when I returned to visit friends on Jackson Street as one who had mounted the ladder of success after overcoming the early years of despair. ***My God, How Great Thou Art!***

At the end of our tremendous excursion, we were glad to return home. The children had survived well with friends and a maid that we had met only a few hours before we departed. Helen still thinks she was an angel. Just before we had departed, our maid suddenly had quit. Someone recommended this lady, and she did an outstanding job. After we returned, she left the house, and we never saw her again.

During the year prior to attending the Outstanding Airman ceremonies, I offered to perform a singing concert to help Father Binua raise funds to build a new church. The concert was a success, and the funds raised were sufficient to build the new edifice named in honor of the Blessed Mother, Mary.

For four years, I had such a rewarding experience, maintaining my spiritual attitude while managing the largest propulsion branch in the Pacific. I assisted in the chapel program, served as rector for a Cursillo weekend, sponsored a young Filipino kid through school, served as master of ceremonies for the Soul Twisters, became a charter member of the Race Relations Committee, president of the school board, lector, cantor, lay Eucharistic minister for the Catholic program, CCD teacher, active member of the Knights of Columbus, official greeter for the first POW returning from Hanoi in February 1973, warm-up show for Bob Hope's last performance in the Pacific and frequent entertainer for the Top Hat NCO Club.

Captain "Fig" Newton approached me one day before I departed from the Philippines and said, "Chief, I am considering applying for the Thunderbirds flying demonstration team." "Why not," I countered. "You are as good a pilot as anyone else in the Air Force." I later learned that he applied and had been accepted. He was the only officer to hold three key positions: Slot Flyer, Narrator and Commander. "Fig" went on to become the third black Four-Star General in the Air Force. We remained friends over the years.

Chito, the young Filipino lad we had adopted, completed his high school studies, and we financed him for one-year of college courses.

Our children enjoyed their stay in the Philippines with involvement in church, school, youth groups, stage shows and Pat became known for directing the high school band. Donna competed in college gymnastics, Carmen did great embroidery, Henri excelled in piano lessons and Bill played football.

When we left in July 1973, we left behind many Filipino friends. The love we shared will live forever. Those four years were the most incredible years of my entire Air Force career. Thanks Dad.

It is a great feeling to know that the boy from Jackson Street will be remembered for the Catholic Church he helped to finance. Merci, mon Pere.

Griffiss Air Force Base – Rome, New York

Our return from the Philippines was different from our earlier return from Japan. Our family did not grow in number over those four years. Our vacation was good. Mother Dubois and Mom had grown close to Rickey while he was attending Pensacola Junior College.

We arrived at Griffiss on a Saturday which was Carl's birthday. We celebrated it at the NCO Club on Sunday after we attended Mass. Tom Dutko greeted me. He wanted to know why he had not seen me at church before. I told him we had just arrived. "That explains it," he retorted. From that simple greeting, Tom and Mary Dutko became our closest friends, even today in 2007.

I was assigned as Maintenance Superintendent for the 49th Fighter Interceptor Squadron. We maintained the squadron for F-106 interceptor fighters. I was there only a short while before being selected to attend the Senior Non-Commissioned Officer Academy (SNCOA).

In November 1973, Father Ariano arrived to become Wing Command Chaplain. After attending his first Mass, I approached him and said, "I think I know you." He answered, "You should, you were at one of my retreats in Japan in 1959." I had attended my first retreat as a newly-converted Catholic with the Holy Name Society in Itazuke, Japan, and Father Ariano was the retreat master. I always remembered what he instructed us to do. "In silence, walk outside and listen to what God has to say to you." It was a great spiritual experience, which I continue to practice even today. It's truly amazing what God can do when we listen to Him. *Love you, Dad.*

On a Saturday just before noon, Staff Sergeant Roebuck, a member of the alert section, came to talk with me. I was briefing Major Strickland and gave Roebuck a "wait-a-moment" sign through the office window. When I finished, I went out to talk with Roebuck, but he was gone. Two days later, he had not reported for work. He failed to answer his telephone. I went to his trailer court only to find, much to my horrible regret, that Roebuck was dead. He had taken his own life with a plastic bag over his head and a GI belt around his neck. That was one of the most difficult situations I had ever had to deal with. I went to the doctor to get help, and I was placed on Valium. This took place before Christmas. I helped prepare the memorial services. Thankfully, I had managed to get into his trailer and had the remains removed before his family returned from a weekend in Rochester, New York.

All my family was home for Christmas. Rick was in his final year of junior college. Pat was a freshman at Florida State University. This was his second choice. While stationed in the Philippines Pat's high school academic grades earned him a Presidential Appointment to West Point. He was rejected because of a skin allergy. After several medical evaluations were unable to reverse the West Point medical board's decision, he enrolled at Florida State University, enlisted in their ROTC program and after four years, graduated as Distinguished Cadet with a regular officer's commission.

Dr. Cole, a friend stationed at Clark, worked with us and with other doctors trying to get Pat cleared of the skin problem. "If they refused to accept Pat after the recommendations of the same physicians who worked with the POWS, it is not God's will for Pat to attend West Point," he reasoned. He was right. That class was the one that washed out for cheating. This is not to say that Pat would have been one, but *My Dad knows best.*

Before the Christmas holidays, the family was invited to have Thanksgiving dinner at Helen's sister's home in Mobile and Bessie Mae prepared a great meal. This was the first time I had met Helen's biological dad, who was in very poor health and living with Bessie Mae.

When I returned to Griffiss, I learned that three black airmen had been incarcerated in Herkimer, New York. I asked if anyone had visited them and was told that no one could visit because they had attacked a police officer and the charge was a felony. I went to Herkimer and the jail officials wanted to know why no one had called to check on those men. They released them but I was instructed to have them back for a court appearance, which I did. At the hearing, the charges were dropped. The judge did restrict them to the base and insisted that they attend Sunday church services. Toward Christmas, Anthony, one of those on restriction, was back in jail.

After Christmas Mass, Father Joe asked what I was going to do? I told him about some people I would visit in the hospital and then go to the jail in Herkimer. He followed me and we were caught in a bad snowstorm. It took hours to get to the jail. The police greeted me and allowed me to deliver cookies Helen had prepared for Anthony. Father Joe realized that he had a dinner appointment and he was late. The people who had invited him learned that he was with me and waited for him. What a joyful time we had tromping through the snow-filled streets in the family housing area singing Christmas carols. This was so different from the warm Christmas in the Philippines.

Rick and Pat returned to college, and I went to the Senior NCO Academy. The class began the second week of January 1974. It was the first time I had returned to Montgomery since leaving in 1949 to enter the Air Force, and what a difference I found. I visited the college campus and found Dr. Hardy still there.

At the end of the second week, after classes were done, a group of us went over to Maxwell AFB to have dinner at the NCO Club. While there, I met Ann who noticed the cross I was wearing. She wanted to know if I would attend their Baptist church and I accepted her invitation. That Sunday I heard the best singing I had heard in years. The choir had over 30 singers and those Baptists sure can perform. I also met Reverend Andrews, the pastor.

During the week, Father Ariano had arrived at Maxwell to attend a Chaplain's course. I told him about Lilly Hill Baptist Church and he should hear the choir. He accepted the invitation and we went together in full uniform. The pastor invited him to be his guest in the pulpit. Moments after the service started, the ushers took up the collection, after which they rolled a casket in front of the altar. I could see the perplexed look on Father Joe's face from where I was sitting.

Starting his sermon, Reverend Andrews told us he was preaching the devil's funeral. At the end of his sermon he asked the ushers to come and open up the casket. He invited all to come and view the devil's body. The pastor took Father Joe by the arm and guided him down in front to the casket. By now, I am crying from laughing so hard. Inside the casket was a large mirror. And everyone who looked inside saw himself or herself. I asked Father Joe how the devil looked. He said, "Walt, he looked too natural." He asked why I didn't go over and view him. I said that I had seen him that morning while I was shaving.

At a Sunday Mass, the priest at Gunter Air Base, where the SNOCA was being held, invited General Flynn as guest speaker. The General was Catholic and had been a POW for over six years. He was not on the aircraft with the returnees I had greeted. He talked about his years as a POW in the "Hanoi Hilton." He spoke about courage and not giving up, adding that his first night had been really tough. The interrogation was severe. The injuries he had suffered after being shot down over Hanoi were minor compared with the torture he had received. Without releasing any pertinent information other than his name and serial number, he had been taken to a cell where his faith had been tested to the limit. This, he said, is when faith has to be real. He cried a lot that night in Hanoi. The next morning he knew that he would have to endure the same torture. While waiting for the North Vietnamese to come to get him, a small sparrow appeared on his window sill. He gained strength from seeing that sparrow, which did not fly away. The Vietnamese soldier came and took him in for more interrogation. The General said he doubted if he could withstand the same amount of torture again. Seated on the same stool that had been kicked out from under him many times before at the first meeting, he sat there waiting and while he was waiting, under the door sill came a small sparrow. His faith was renewed ("His eye is on the sparrow, and I know He watches me."). The North Vietnamese officer asked him if he had told him everything that he knew. The General said, "Yes." Without a lick or a slap to the face, he was taken back to his cell.

His message was that it took faith to survive those torturous years. And prisoners who did not have faith did not make it. His message was very touching.

When we talked at length after the service, I really wanted to get him to come to Griffiss, but it never happened. I did tell his story of faith during several of my lectures.

The curriculum at the SNOC Academy was not yet fully organized since our class was only the second one to go through the course. We played a lot of volleyball and over the 6 weeks, I lost 20 pounds. Helen's dad passed away while I was in Montgomery. I went to Mobile to be with the family since Helen would be unable to attend the funeral services.

The night our class graduated, Elvis Presley was performing in downtown Montgomery and I was asked to sing. Some attending the graduation dinner said I did well considering the downtown competition.

Helen was glad to have me home, saying she had shoveled more snow than she ever wanted to.

In April after I returned, Father Joe and I formed the very first Cursillo class at Rome, New York. The base allowed us to use space above the Base Flight section. We had 20 men attending, including a Circuit Judge and a Protestant minister. The evening of the Cursillo, the Strategic Air Command (SAC) Operational Readiness Inspection (ORI) team arrived on base. The whistle blew hours before the Cursillo weekend was to start. The candidates still came. No one called to have them report to duty. The class was moving along well. The men were entering into this deeper encounter with Jesus. I was the Rector and Father Joe was the Spiritual Director.

On Saturday evening we heard the B-52 Bombers revving up their engines preparing for take off. This would be the *pass-or-fail-portion* of the ORI. The men in the Cursillo prayed for the safety of the aircrews. The Command Chaplain for SAC, traveling with the ORI team had been stationed with me in the Philippines. He had made his weekend over there and knew about the Cursillo weekend because I had written him a letter asking him to come and be a team member. When his aircraft arrived, he wanted to know where he could find Walt Richardson and where the Cursillo weekend was being held. He found us and instead of spending time with the inspection team, he helped us with the Cursillo.

At midnight, I heard people moving about downstairs in the flight kitchen. I inquired and learned that the bomber crews had completed their mission and all had returned safely The Cursillo weekend was a total spiritual success. Every candidate committed himself to the work of Jesus. Before the class ended, it was suggested that the team and the candidates make a poster and send it to the Wing Commander in appreciation for not canceling the weekend services. They did. Father Joe and I delivered it to Colonel Maxson, Wing Commander, who said he had known about the Cursillo weekend and had decided to let it go on knowing how much planning had taken place. We told him we had prayed for the combat team. He told us our prayers were answered because for the first time ever, his aircrew had made a perfect bomb run and had passed the ORI with an outstanding rating, something that had not happened previously in the wing. During the weekend, I met Frank Winslow, who had helped out and became a real good friend.

The Base Commander was Colonel Gilbert. His wife, Jeannie, a very devout Catholic, befriended Helen while we were still living in guest quarters. Jeannie laundered our clothes at her quarters. When Jeannie became very sick, the Catholic prayer group did a full night vigil outside of her intensive care unit. Colonel Gilbert was not into all that we were doing but he never turned us away. Jeannie recovered and she wanted to attend a Cursillo, but the practice is that the husband goes first and then the wife. There was no way we would get Colonel Gilbert to consent to attend a weekend.

The Gilbert's boys were at Mass the last weekend we spent at Griffiss. Frank Winslow was hosting a farewell cookout for our family at his quarters on the lake. I invited the Gilbert's boys while their mother was still in the hospital. They went to get permission from their dad. While waiting for them, Helen and I continued cleaning the quarters in preparation for departure. The boys arrived with Colonel Gilbert who asked, "Chief, am I invited?" Of course, I said yes. He attended, and, while he was there, Frank Winslow told him that he also would attend a Cursillo weekend. Colonel Gilbert did not protest. He did say that he was not a Catholic. Frank asserted, "I will take care of that," and did. Colonel Tom Gilbert became a Catholic, and he and Jeannie (who had recovered) had their marriage blessed by Father Joe. I learned thereafter that Colonel Gilbert would open his staff meetings with a prayer. Most importantly, Tom and I became very close friends. Jeannie made a Cursillo; so did Tom.

For three months I sang for the Shriners. Karl Zech heard about my singing and requested that I sing for their Ladies' Nights, and I did. The Squadron received numerous letters commending us for entertaining them.

Our family did increase. We purchased a poodle. Little Bit integrated into the family and played a major role for over 14 years until he died.

Helen and I got involved with network marketing. We began building our business. The group we were a part of was in Syracuse, New York. It wasn't long after we got involved that my singing voice was used for functions. I sang "*The Impossible Dream*" at the request of Richard Devos, co-founder of Amway Corporation the book, "Jonathan Livingston Seagull" was the book offered to the sale force. Throughout the year I sang at many other functions.

Airman Anthony finally was released from the service. He just could not blend in. The last episode took place one Sunday when I visited his room in the barracks. He took a long time to open the door. When I entered, I asked how he was doing and he said okay. I heard noises and I wanted to know if someone else was in the room. He said no. Later the noise came again. Inside Anthony's wall locker was his pregnant girlfriend. I escorted the young lady to a bus homeward bound and within a week she delivered the baby. Although Anthony could not make it in the Air Force, he still had high regards for me.

The year at Griffiss had really been a busy one. The church sponsored a family retreat in the beautiful Adirondacks which the whole family attended. Bertha, my favorite, came from Pensacola, Florida to New York and attended the retreat with us. We spent a week together.

I was guest speaker for the American Legion Fourth of July celebration. Nominated for Senior Enlisted Advisor of the Air Defense Command. I was Council Chairman for the Boy Scouts, and a choir member, George Laubmeier, who directed our choir, became a close friend. He accompanied me for special singing engagements including the installation dinner for the Potentate of the Ziyra Shrine. We spent our last night at Tom and Mary's home.

Once again, the boy from Jackson Street was instrumental in bridging the racial gap that had existed in the squadron regarding the situation with the three black airmen. Law enforcement officers felt that those airmen had been forsaken. Indeed, it was racially tinted because the police officer with whom they had fought was white. The friendly approach, while working out the details, and the willingness to cooperate with the powers involved, smoothed out the wrinkles caused by racial differences. Our departure left memories we would never return to recapture. ***How Great Thou Art!***

Amazing Grace

Udorn, Thailand

While attending the Senior Non-Commissioned Officer Academy (SNCOA), I was notified that I would be assigned to Udorn, Thailand in July, 1974. Upon completion of SNCOA, I returned to Griffiss, New York and enjoyed the faith community we had built through the Cursillo Movement and the Life in the Spirit seminars. I attended my first charismatic prayer service in Syracuse, New York. The experiences were different between the Cursillo and the Life Spirit Seminar, but they complemented each other. That year in New York gave me the opportunity to use this beautiful gift of singing for many organizations and special functions. It was a short tour but most rewarding spiritually. I had reunited with Father Ariano, a relationship which would last over the years.

While we were both attending courses at Maxwell Air Force Base, Montgomery, Alabama we took a trip to Florida over a long weekend. We paid a surprise visit to Pat who was a freshman at Florida State University. We enjoyed the day together and I later learned that before we had arrived that Saturday, Pat was about to leave college. We inspired him to continue. He did and graduated Distinguished Cadet of his ROTC class and gained a regular commission in the U.S. Army.

The family moved back into the home we had purchased before I went to Vietnam. This was their second time to live there. I had never lived in this home, having only visited between assignments to Vietnam and the Philippines.

I arrived in Thailand and was assigned to Mac Thai as maintenance superintendent. Our squadron was used to train Laos pilots. Serious discipline problems existed in the units. Unfortunately, it was not the young airmen but the senior NCOs who were the culprits. Most of them were over-indulging in alcohol. The initiation into the tiger club required getting so drunk that one couldn't remember what had taken place. I spoke out against this practice, but afterwards they plotted to have me removed from their unit. They succeeded. While home on Christmas leave, they were able to get me transferred to the F-4 Fighter Wing.

I arrived at Udorn a month before Father Hernandez. Before leaving for the Philippines, we had attended Mass at the Chapel at Travis Air Force Base, California. We knew Father Borre, one of the priests assigned there, and had gone to attend his Mass and to meet with him. Father Borre spent time with us after Mass. It turned out that Father Hernandez was there, too, but did not come to introduce himself. When he arrived in Thailand, he told me on that Sunday, he had prophesied, "Someday I will be with that man."

We became very close friends. He was aware of the problems I was dealing with in the squadron where I was assigned.

One of the F-4 pilots stationed there was "Chappie," James' son. I contacted him and requested an appointment. He invited me to his quarters. I introduced myself and told him that we were related. He looked surprised and asked how. I said that his grandmother had helped raise me. I told him about attending her private school. He asked about things he had always wanted to know which I shared with him. Afterwards, we continued to talk with each other until he rotated.

Christmas was approaching, and I told Father Hernandez that I was going to spend Christmas with my family. He wanted to know how I was traveling. I said, *"I am flying united."* He wanted to know if my reservations were out of Bangkok. I said, *"No, I am flying united with Jesus,"* meaning, I was going to fly home, space available.

Before leaving Udorn, the President of the Chase Manhattan Bank, located on base – a recent convert into the Catholic faith – asked me to be his Godfather. I did. Before I left, he called me into his office and asked how much money I needed to get home. I told him I was flying space available. He told his loan officer to write me a loan for three hundred dollars, explaining he didn't want me to be stranded somewhere and unable to get home in time for Christmas. I took the check.

The first stop out of Thailand was Guam. A priest friend from Griffiss, whom Father Joe had replaced, was stationed there. He came to the terminal and offered me room at his home overnight. That next morning he left his quarters early because one of the B-52 Bombers had crashed shortly after takeoff and there were no survivors. At noon, I attended Mass with Father Martin Cain, Wing Chaplain, who had been stationed with us in Dover, Delaware. In fact, our son Bill was named William Martin after him. He stayed with me until my flight departed Guam.

When I arrived at Travis, I learned that the Navy had a flight to Pensacola, Florida, but I had to get there by bus with a stop in Oakland, California. Standing there waiting for the bus, fear came upon me. Here I was standing on a crowded corner in California in my uniform and felt afraid. The fear was justified, moments later a military person came and directed me to a safer place because someone had been attacked where I was waiting. Thanks Dad.

The flight to Pensacola was smooth. I arrived home in time to take care of Helen, who had been ill for several days. The Christmas visit was great.

As usual, I was attending daily Mass at St. Mary Catholic Church. I remained after Mass to pray. I was saying my Rosary when a lady approached me and laid a blue book on the pew near me, never spoke, just turned and left the church. She did put her name inside the cover. I picked up the prayer booklet and discovered it was the 15 prayers of St. Bridget, who always wanted to know how many wounds Jesus had suffered during his Passion. He revealed to her that he had suffered **5,475** wounds during the scourging. And, he said, if she wished to honor them, to pray 15 Our Fathers and Hail Marys each day for one year, and then pray the prayer he had taught her and, in doing so, she would have honored each of his wounds.

I looked through the booklet and discovered a novena prayer to St. Therese, the little flower. It promised that this **novena** never fails. Simply, pray 24 Glory Be's to the Father each day and ask for St. Therese to intercede for you and state what you want.

I knew I wanted a flight back to Thailand. So, I read the instructions and started my novena prayers that very moment. I continued until the day I was ready to leave. The night before my departure, I called several locations trying to find a flight to California. The only one available was leaving out of Pensacola Naval Air Station on Sunday morning. I prayed my novena prayer and asked St. Therese to help me find a flight. After Mass, Helen and I were to take off for Pensacola. Hurlburt Field was near our home, only about three miles away. I said I am going to check here and see if there was a flight to California. Helen reminded me that I had checked the night before, and they had nothing going to the west coast.

When I entered the Base Operation section, I asked if there was any flight going west. They answered, "Yes, in fact we are making flight plans right now. Where in California do you want to go?" I said, "Travis," and they rearranged their flight plans to give me a ride to Travis. I went out and told Helen that I was on my way. While flying I thanked St. Therese. She had arranged for me to have a private flight to California. While flying, the inspiration came back to me that whenever a favor is granted, St. Therese always sends a rose. She told me during my silent moments in prayer that my rose would be in a small vase near the tabernacle in the Blessed Sacrament Chapel in Udorn where I had spent hours praying and communicating with my Dad.

When I arrived in California, an announcement came over the PA system asking for anyone desiring space-available travel to Guam, to please report to the counter. I went and, within one hour I was again in flight, this time on my way to Guam. (Therese travels fast.)

When I arrived in Hawaii, I visited personnel because I had received a call while home on leave that I had been transferred from Mac Thai. I learned that my new assignment was with the fighter wing.

The flight plan changed from Guam to the Philippines. This is really where I wanted to go because daily flights left the Philippines to Udorn, Thailand.

Since I had been blessed and St. Therese had done a great job getting me this far, I decided to remain over night in the Philippines to visit with friends we had left there. I learned that a Cursillo class was starting in Apalat. I used a friend's car and drove to the Cursillo. A number of the brothers who had helped me were there on the team. Brother Nanny was there. I went in and prayed with them and excused myself because I had to get my flight back to Thailand.

The next morning I arrived at Udorn, went to the barracks, off loaded my luggage and ran to the chapel. And there it was just as I had envisioned it during my flight from Hurlburt to California, a fresh-picked rose in a small vase near the Blessed Sacrament tabernacle. This was the beginning of many roses I would receive from my little saint, Therese. From that humble first Novena, I have never ceased to pray it everyday since 1974. I also prayed the 15 prayers of St. Bridget for 9 straight years. *"Amazing Grace."*

Early the next morning, I heard the voice of the Lord speaking to me. He said, *"Go back to the Philippines and attend the Cursillo."* Initially, I protested saying, "Lord, I have been gone over 30 days, I cannot get any more time off." He said, *"Go back to the Philippines."* I went to my commander and asked if I could go to the Philippines for the weekend and attend a retreat. He granted me permission to leave. When I arrived, I did not have military orders to enter the country. A call was placed back to my unit and the commander approved my being there.

I went directly to the Cursillo, told the leader (Rector) that I would spend the night in the Blessed Sacrament Chapel praying for the men going through during that weekend. It was late that night when a Filipino gentlemen entered the chapel and began crying. It was dark inside and he could not see me in the back of the chapel. He continued praying and crying. I listened for a while before I made a move to go comfort him. I left my back row pew and went up front to console him. I approached the man and took him in my arms and said, *"God loves you and so do I."* There was sufficient light to show the shocked look on his face. I released him and returned to my back row pew and continued my prayers throughout the rest of the night and enjoyed time with my father, God.

During the closing ceremony, the leaders of the team asked if anyone had an experience they wished to share. A gentleman was allowed to get up and tell his story. I did not recognize him, and he did not know me. He could not speak English so he was granted permission to speak in Tagala. He began to speak very animatedly. Somewhere along in his story, everyone began to laugh. I laughed too, although I didn't know what he was saying.

Shortly afterwards, he said something that really caused everyone to roll in laughter. I laughed too. Then one Filipino gentleman asked if I knew what he said. I replied in the negative. He told me that the man had shared with them about his life and how he had protested going to the Cursillo. He said his friends had tricked him into coming. He spoke about how angry he was when he learned it was about Christian love and forgiving. He went on to say that for two days he just wanted to get it over with and get out of there. For over 18 years he had been out of the church and had not been a part of any of the sacraments. On that day, he had finally decided to open his heart and had gone to confession. The priest told him to go into the Blessed Sacrament Chapel and pray to God and listen to him. He went. While he was crying, I had come up and held him in my arms. He said he had been praying to God that if he really loved him and forgave him his sins, to please take him into his arms and tell him so, and this is precisely when I was holding and telling him that *God loved him*. The group laughed. And then he said, **"I didn't know God was black."** This is what really caused the greater laughter. After the closing Mass, I went to him and I had someone interpret for me *that God is of many colors, this is why we have the rainbow.*

I returned to Thailand, knowing that this was why God had continued to call me and had arranged for me to get back to the Philippines. *Amazing Grace.*

At a cookout after Mass, I shared my story with the men who gathered there about my trip home for the holidays and how I had traveled *united with Jesus*. I told them I had prayed for St. Therese's intercession and about the fresh rose. Across from me was a young airman; you could see his expression change with a growing smile as he listened to me. He said, "Chief, I placed that rose there." I thanked him. He asked if I wanted to know why he had done it. I said, "Yes." He told the group that before he left home to come to Thailand that his wife had asked for a divorce. He left praying that she would not leave him. On that day, he received a letter from his wife saying that she had talked with a priest who enlightened her and encouraged her to keep their marriage together. She closed by saying how much she loved him. He took the letter and went to the chapel to pray and, as he was about to enter the chapel, a rose on a trellis fell right in front of him. Of course, he wanted to give God something beautiful, so he plucked that rose and placed it in a vase near the Blessed Sacrament. I wrote his wife and told her the story. She replied that she would keep their love and marriage together. Thanks Dad.

The new assignment had its challenges. The Wing was experiencing more than its share of engine compressor damages and really needed help to correct the problem. Colonel Kowanomi, Chief of Maintenance, assigned me to look into the situation. During the first weekend on duty, I took the Colonel's vehicle and toured the flight line. This was something my predecessor had never done. He spent 12 hours each day in the office and never visited the troops on the flight line.

While I was inspecting the area, I noticed an airman coming out of the intake of an F-4. I waited until he got out and asked why he had entered the intake without wearing the protection overalls. He held up a dirty pair of coveralls and I realized why he would not put them on. I took those unserviceable overalls to the flight line supervisor and asked where the serviceable overalls were. He couldn't provide any. I gave him until close of business to have clean overalls for his people and no one was to enter the intake without wearing them. This was the beginning of the reduction of foreign-object damages to the engines.

When I arrived back at the office, the Chief of Maintenance called me into his office and asked if I had been on the flight line. I responded that I had. He allowed that he had already heard that I had ordered them to get serviceable overalls. I again admitted I did. He was pleased.

On Monday, following my visit on the flight line, the Squadron Maintenance Officer came into my office and said I should report to his office before I went out on his flight line. I said, "Major, I can do that. But I will first take your demand up with the Colonel who instructed me to go out and make an unannounced inspection. He will want to know why one of his Majors has more power and authority than he does." I continued, "Wait a moment and I will let him know you are here." The officer replied, "Just forget it." I insisted that he speak with the Colonel, since he had a problem with me visiting the flight line and doing my job. Perhaps the Colonel would like to change his mind.

We never entered the Colonel's office. I did tell the Colonel about the incident. The Squadron superintendent was a very prejudiced individual. Serious racial incidents were going on in the flight line unattended. I was told by the Colonel to check out the complaints about racial turmoil

120

in the Squadron. I went down and talked with the black airmen, and they shared with me what was going on. One airman I knew had a very hot temper and he was the target. They would entice him into heated discussions to get him angry enough to cause a fight. When I learned what was going on, I had this airman come into my office and vent his frustration. One Sunday evening it happened. He and a white sergeant got into a fight. The Air Police placed the black airman in jail and did nothing to the white sergeant. I took Father Hernandez and we went to the Air Police security section where they had the black airman confined. Father Hernandez requested that the Squadron Commander be contacted. The Commander was unaware of what had taken place and requested that the black airman be released.

Later that evening, a meeting was held in my office. The Wing Vice Commander said, *"Chief, I heard that you have sufficient influence to cause a riot if you wanted to."* I was stung by his comment and asked him to repeat it, which he did. The next morning once again, I wrote a letter of resignation and addressed copies to all of the important General officers I knew, including the Chief of Staff of the Air Force. The Wing Commander learned of my intentions and asked that I not mail the letters, and he would take care of the situation. The Vice Commander was transferred. It would be him or me. One of us had to leave the command after such a ridiculous remark.

The Wing Commander asked me to form a social action committee and gather the young airmen together and discuss their problems. We organized a committee similar to the one formed in the Philippines when we were experiencing racial problems. It worked. One reason I was able to gain the proper respect was because the higher officials knew that I had a very close friend in Lieutenant General LeRoy Manor, Commander of 13th Air Force of which this Wing was part. The General was a very devout Catholic. I had met him several times at Mass before I departed the Philippines. Whenever he visited Udorn, he would request a meeting with me. A great gentleman, he did not want me to express any problems going on at the base. Instead, he was more interested in me and my family whom he had come to know while we were stationed together.

The airman confined for fighting continued to come into my office and vent his anger. I would talk with him. He expressed how hard it was holding back from the verbal attacks he was experiencing. I coached him until it was time for him to rotate. He was able to transfer back to the states with all of his stripes. He wept as he was about to board the aircraft departing Thailand. He said that I was the very first male in his life that showed him love. We cried together. *Thanks Dad.*

During the last eight months at Udorn, Father Hernandez and I conducted four Cursillo weekends. We started in August 1974 with only six men attending daily Mass and after four Cursillos, in July, 1975, there were over 50 men attending daily Mass. Bishop Duhart, Bishop of Udorn, was very impressed. He would give talks during our Cursillo weekends. He became a very close friend. When I was about to rotate, he gave a dinner for Father Hernandez and me at one of the nice restaurants in Udorn. He learned that I was transferring to Eglin Air Force Base and would be right at home and Father Hernandez was being assigned to Tyndall, only about 80 miles away. He renamed us MOWOGs (Manipulators of the Will of God).

The Wing's bad experience with foreign object damages to engines dropped to zero. The young airmen were provided clean overalls to wear when entering the aircraft intakes. The morale on the flight line was much better.

Gladly, I provided entertainment at the base club and was contracted to sing once a month. Father Hernandez attended one performance. A sergeant with his Thai girlfriend kept heckling me and wanted me to sing a song I had not prepared to do, so I turned to the band and asked them to play a different song for the sergeant. I sang *Your Cheating Heart*, and Father Hernandez said he noticed the sergeant slide down into his chair and had nothing else to say.

We announced a Cursillo weekend to be held near the border of Laos. One airman went but was not really interested in the religious stuff. Knowing where we had scheduled the Cursillo, we were sternly briefed by the Base Commander **not** to leave the compound because hostile activities were going on. We instructed the candidates not to leave the grounds. The location was beautiful and suitable for a good retreat.

Mio tribesmen and their families had settled in this small portion of Thailand when they were forced out of Laos because of their activities with the U.S. Government. Extremely poor and helpless, the church where we were, provided them with rice and some medical supplies.

They were dying off rapidly. The priest mentioned to me that they were very devout Catholics. He requested that I sing the *Ave Maria* for them during Mass on Sunday. I did.

The first night talks went well. The next morning we discovered that one of the airmen, named Richard, was missing. We had strict orders not to leave the compound and could not go look for him. Father Hernandez joined me as we prayed the rosary for the airman's safety.

Later that morning he returned, bringing with him a Thai gentleman. I asked him to join me inside and I told him that the Thai person had to leave. He protested and said if he went so would he. Father Hernandez had turned the situation over to me so I talked with him. I took this airman into the chapel, and we prayed together. He turned to me and said that on the previous night he could not stand the silence. He left and had spent the night talking with the Thai gentleman he had with him. He said please let me show him our Buddha. I granted him that request. He took the man inside the church and pointed to Jesus on the cross and said to him, "That's my Buddha." The Thai gentleman left without protest. The airman was granted permission to remain throughout the weekend. He found the true love of Jesus Christ in those last two days. His testimony during the closing ceremony was great. When we returned to the base, he wrote to his mother. He told her about his encounter with Jesus Christ. He gave his mother my name and address. She wrote and told me how she had prayed that her children would come to accept Jesus in their lives. She was associated with John Kennedy's family and had helped during his campaign for President of the United States. She went on to write that when traveling she would find a chapel in the airport and spend time meditating. She wanted to meet me. She offered to pray for me for what we had done for her son. Years later, I received letters from Richard.

Richard's mother was not the only letters I received. Many wives wrote to tell me how beautiful we had made their husbands and thanked me for sharing the Father's love with them. One declared, "He is simply beautiful." *Amazing Grace.*

When my departure date was announced to leave Udorn, the superintendent that I considered prejudiced wanted to host a farewell party for me. I declined. I knew it was not from the heart, yet still a friendly gesture. I departed on an early morning flight with only a friend and Father Hernandez there to bid me farewell. Thanks Dad.

Back to Eglin <u>Again!</u>

If I Can Help Somebody

You may remember that Mom's favorite saying was "never burn bridges behind you because you never know when you will have to back up". When I received orders returning me to Eglin Air Force Base after 17 years, I was very excited. Finally, I would be living in the home we had purchased when I was assigned to Vietnam. I returned at the top rung of the non-com ladder as a **Chief Master Sergeant**. I found that a few of the civilians I had worked with were still there.

It was while attending Mass during a Holy Day of Obligation that Mr. Brantley, with whom I had worked as a quality control inspector before departing for Japan in 1958, caught up with me after Mass to congratulate me. He said he knew even then that I would make it to the top (with God's undivided help).

Assigned to the 33rd Fighter Wing, I was disappointed to find racial problems still existing. A young black airman assigned to my section as an administrator, seemed to have his future under attack. I made mental notes of the extra expectations required of him.

The flight line was busy. After the flying was over, we spent many hours in clearing up discrepancies generated during flights. One evening after a busy day of flying, the line was full of broken F-4 aircraft. The day shift supervisors had left to gather at Duffy's, a small club near the squadron. I went over there and requested that they return to the flight

124

line until the workload could be handled by the evening shift. At that moment, I did nothing to enhance my popularity. Again, I was the first black chief master to be in charge of the flight line. This was no different from Udorn as I could feel the resentment coming from most of the white NCOs that worked for me.

As the weeks and months passed, it became obvious that neither the senior NCOs nor the officers were accepting my presence in the organization favorably. It did not matter because I knew what needed to be done, and I would accept nothing less . . . *Be with me, Dad.*

Approaching the Christmas holidays, I asked the Squadron Commander if there was a breakdown of the personnel needed to cover the holidays. He did not have an answer. I asked him who knew the answer and he referred me to the Chief of Maintenance. From him, I requested the same information but he, too, was unable to provide an answer. I was told that if I needed an answer I should ask the Wing Commander. I made an appointment, went and talked with the Wing Commander, and again I was disappointed with the answer. I explained to him that I had promised the troops that I would have an answer for them at the Monday morning formation. He said to tell them he had not yet decided. It was not the answer I wanted, but I reported exactly what he said.

A few days later, I was notified that I was being transferred. I requested to speak once again with the Wing Commander, hoping I might get out of the new assignment. He said the special orders transferring me had come down from Tactical Air Command, and there was nothing he could do about it. I was not convinced that he was helpless, considering the ample power invested in Wing Commanders.

Assigned to Tactical Warfare Center, my new job had nothing to do with working directly with aircraft or with young airmen. This, I truly detested. I later learned that the official word was out that I was not allowed to visit the 33rd for any reason at all except to get required reports. During those visits, I was not to have any contact with the young black airmen. So be it for desiring to *help somebody*. I had momentarily forgotten that I had returned to the base where I had first encountered the greatest discrimination in my entire military career.

I had been away from the 33rd Fighter Wing for a short while when I learned that the young airman who had worked for me was being targeted and charged with "failure to repair." He was accused of abusing his lunch hour and I was aware that the plot was to catch him acting out of order. I had placed a sign-out board in the office instructing everyone to sign in and out. I kept records of those following the instructions, particularly noting the failure of the officer assigned. When the charges were raised against that young airman, I took my documented log of those failing to follow orders to sign in and out to the legal officer handling the charges. The charges against that young airman were dropped. He was able to finish his regular tour of duty and discharged honorably . . . *Thanks Dad.*

Well, I realized that in spite of the intervening years, the prejudices were still here. However, this time I was in a position with sufficient rank that I could speak out, and I did. I totally disliked the job I was assigned to in TAWC. Placed in a technical sergeant's position, I merely ran reports from one section to the other, attended boring meetings and watched people work crossword puzzles.

The only consolation of being assigned to Eglin was being home with my family. The children were entering their teenage years, and I was needed at home to help them through those most challenging times. Rick was attending college in Arizona, Pat was at Florida State University, Lillie was a senior in high school, Carmen was a junior, Donna and Henri were two years behind Carmen and Bill a year behind Donna. All 5 of them were heading toward graduation and hoping to attend college, which they did . . . *Thanks, Dad.*

After I became active at St. Mary Catholic Church as the cantor for the early Sunday morning Mass, I received in the mail an invitation to attend an ordination to the priesthood. I was surprised when I opened the letter and discovered that it was from Henry Petter, with whom I had served in the Philippines. He and I had entertained a lot together. Henry was extremely talented, playing both the harmonica and the guitar simultaneously. He had attended the Cursillo while stationed there. Inviting me to attend the ordination, he requested that I sing. Guess what? ***"How Great Thou Art."***

After the Mass was over, Father Petter gave blessings to those who wanted to receive them. As I knelt before him, he laid hands on me and said that it was on the weekend that I invited him to attend Cursillo that he made up his mind to return to the seminary. I felt warm all over.

Just to think that I had made that kind of impression upon him. Later, it was an honor to be invited to his silver jubilee in Plano, Texas.

To keep myself together while working at TAWC, I would attend daily Mass and after work go to the chapel and pray. I spent hours alone in the Blessed Sacrament Chapel. There were evenings when I had to find a door left unlocked through which to enter. I never failed to get in, but finally, the priest gave me a key to the door. So I was able to get in any time I wanted to.

One evening while I was praying, a young couple entered the chapel. I was kneeling up front and did not look back to see who had come in, but I could hear someone crying. I finished my prayers and offered to help if I could. The young lady was on active duty, but the fellow was not. I asked what I could do to help them. She wanted to know if I was a chaplain. I said no, but I could get one for them. I asked what the problem was. She said they wanted to get married. I asked if they had planned this and did they have legal paperwork to get married, and I got "yes" to both questions. I asked why they needed to get married this evening. She said they had been scheduled to be at the Justice of the Peace's office but when they arrived late, he would not perform the marriage. I asked to see their paperwork. "Follow me," I said, and they went with me to see Reverend Williams. He was located downtown near my home. I told Reverend Williams what had happened and asked if he would perform the marriage. He said that he would but wanted to know why they needed to do this so quickly. The young lady explained that she was on a military exercise and her supervisor had given her an hour to go get married and back to work. *This was that Mighty 33rd* and, after all, she was a Black airman.

Reverend Williams said we needed another witness so I went home, got Helen, returned and then the ceremony started. When Reverend Williams came to the part in the ceremony to exchange rings, they had none. Helen shed her rings and the ceremony went on. Our children knew what was going on because we had told them what was happening. When we arrived back home, they greeted the young couple with grains of rice. Helen asked if they would stay and have their first dinner with us. I called her commander, told him where she was, that they had gotten married and were about to sit down for dinner. I asked him to grant her an extra hour, which he did. The young man had already purchased his bus ticket back to North Carolina. He, too, had pressing commitments to meet but the most important part was done; they were married! They didn't get to spend the first night together.

Years later, I was filling up at the service station at Eglin, and a young man ran up to me saying, "You don't know who I am, do you?" I answered, "You are right. Help me." He recapped the story about their wedding, and they had already spent over six loving years with each other. He expressed how grateful he was for what I had done and for a long time they had wanted to let me know how much they appreciated it . . . *If I can help somebody.*

In September, 1975, I received a telephone call from Father Hernandez. He and his mother had arrived at Tyndall. We planned a meeting at my home, and he came alone. When my family was gathered together and we had gone through the introductions, he shared how I had placed my whole career on the line for that airman that had been locked up for fighting. He explained how different it was after I left. The young airmen had no other senior black NCO to turn to. We relived the days together and our friendly relationship with Bishop Duhart. Father Hernandez said that the Bishop was planning to visit the United States and would come visit me. This he did.

Toward the end of the year, the Bishop of Pensacola-Tallahassee Diocese made the announcement that a Deacon Formation Class would start in 1976. He requested for those men interested in this vocation to make it known to the Diocese. I applied and in January 1976, we held our first meeting with the Bishop. Several meetings and interviews would follow that first meeting.

Father Hernandez and I did not waste any time forming a Cursillo class. In March, 1976, the Bishop approved the first one for the Diocese. It was held at Eglin Base Chapel. Thirteen men attended, most of who had also answered the call to become deacons. For me at TAWC, the years continued to pass on mostly unproductive. I was praying to get transferred but God had other plans. I have learned over the years that my Father, God, keeps the best secrets. My faith was in complete control of my future.

In May 1976, Rick graduated from Arizona State University. Our first child completing college was an indescribably happy moment for us. Yet, I was disappointed when I prepared to attend Mass on Saturday evening following the graduation. Rick had no interest in going with us. Instead, he had planned to attend a graduation party. I insisted that he go to Mass. He was unhappy all through the service. Afterwards, I went with him to the party, and I was really upset. He knew it.

The next morning we departed for the airport without calling Rick to let him know the time of our flight. When he did arrive, I told him how disappointed I had been with his attitude at Mass. He said I had made him feel very bad. He wanted to explain how hard he had worked to finish college in four years, and he felt I had not recognized his efforts. I remained silent. Helen was crying, and we departed.

Still upset when we got home, I was thinking that he had allowed his college education to supersede his Christian obligations.

The following week I was instructed to go to Luke Air Force Base on a special assignment. Tempe is located a few miles from Luke Air Force Base and I knew that God had arranged this trip for me to reconcile with Rick. I called and told him that I was coming and would like to talk with him. He was so happy. When he arrived, we met in the parking lot, embraced each other, and cried for a while. I asked for forgiveness, and he welcomed our resolve. We had lunch together, and he returned to Tempe, Arizona. I had allowed myself to lose sight of all that Rick had done to earn his degree. He loved music so much, he lost interest in his degree of cross-cultural communications and started his music career. Tempe, Flagstaff, Tucson, Phoenix and many surrounding areas would come to love Walt Richardson and his music. We never had another misunderstanding the rest of our years together; in fact, he became my spiritual director. I still call Rick when I need uplifting. He's a great guy. The assignment at TAWC was exceedingly useful after all . . . *Thanks, Dad.*

During the bicentennial year of 1976, Philadelphia, the city of brotherly love, was selected for the 41st Eucharistic Congress. Catholics from all over the world came together for observance. Jerry and Kathy Ottinger, both new graduates from our first Cursillo in our Diocese, and I drove there to attend those four awesome days. There we would be in the company of more Priests, Bishops, Cardinals and Religious than any other place other than, I would say, in heaven. I attended lectures listening to speakers such as Mother Teresa, Dorothy Day, Bishop Sheen, Cardinal Renze of Africa, and my own Chief of Chaplains,

General Meade. Yes, he was there as was Bishop Duhart, and we enjoyed visiting with each other. The most inspiring evening was the Black Cultural Mass. The drum ceremony lasted 30 minutes before the services began. The music was simply great. Tens of thousands of people attended every Mass.

On the first Friday of August, Bishop Sheen gave the homily on the Blessed Virgin Mary. He closed his talk with these words. "If you have had a devotion to the Blessed Mother and you were to die and come to heaven, when St. Peter takes you to introduce you to The Lord, He will say in reply, " Oh, yes, I know, I have heard my mother speak well of you." At that moment, every soul in Soldier's Stadium sprang up and applauded for at least 15 minutes. I was able to maneuver my way through the crowd and made it to the ground level to shake hands with him. He did not remember me. It had been a long time since the speaking engagement when he had come to Delaware, where I had been instrumental in getting him there. But to me it was still a great joy to shake his hand. On Saturday, a grand ultreya was held in Robin Hood Amphitheater where over ten thousand Cursillistas attended.

Before I left Florida to attend the Congress, Father Hernandez gave me a bag full of rosaries saying that the Holy Spirit would guide me to the ones who should receive them. Well, it happened, I went to visit with my sister Bernice who lived in Philadelphia. I arrived at the Mass that evening without talking to the family with which I was living. I knew they would be attending the Mass. When the Mass was over, and I started roaming through the vast number of people, I finally noticed three nuns and I thought they would be my first rosary prospects. As I greeted them and told them why I was giving them the rosaries, I looked to my left and there stood the family I was looking for. *Thanks, Dad.*

During the evening in Robin Hood Park, I was lying on the grass praying my rosary when suddenly I heard a voice saying, can we pray with you? Much to my surprise, it was Colonel Gilbert from Rome, New York. He and Doug, his son, stayed with me and we prayed the rosary together. This was the first time I had seen Colonel Gilbert since he had attended the Cursillo in Rome and had embraced this crazy life we were all so excited about. The next day, Sunday, we met and attended the final Mass together. After returning home, the news broke that several lives were lost due to Legionnaire's Disease while staying in Philadelphia.

Jerry and Kathy gave me a gift for inviting them to come and share my friend's home with them, a beautiful statue of the Blessed Virgin Mary they had purchased while attending the Congress. On the way home the first night out on the return trip, I refused to sleep in the motel; I spent the night in the car with my new gift.

Oh, by the way, the church near where I was staying was St. Therese. They had a life-like statue of the Little Flower and I was able to do my daily devotion there until we departed.

In November 1977, I recorded my first album, "*Christmas Favorites,*" by Walt Richardson. The recording studio was reserved for four hours. Prior to recording, I went to my favorite chapel to pray. The statue of the Blessed Virgin's curtains was drawn. I opened them and at the foot of the statue was a fresh picked rose. This was a gift from St. Therese inspiring me to sing my very best. I did. The first song on the album was dedicated to the Blessed Mother, the "*Ave Maria.*" After four hours, I had recorded 12 songs. I completed the recording in one sitting. The album was released weeks before Christmas. Helen and I spent long hours preparing mail orders. The sales were great. We sold all of the 500 we ordered.

When the officer who had invited the "Soul Twisters" to Guam and later assigned to Tactical Air War Command (TAWC), learned of my recording, he published the information in the Air Force Times. Many airmen and officers I had served with read the article and ordered albums.

This was the year Lillie graduated from high school. She had a great year. Starting out very shy, she overcame that problem and became involved in school activities. While we were stationed in the Philippines, she had oral surgery and wore braces for over a year and when she recovered, she was no longer shy. A beautiful girl, she let loose by being the first black girl to become a cheerleader at Fort Walton Beach High School. When she entered junior college she kept pursuing her cheering activities.

In 1977, Wayne Patrick graduated from Florida State University as Distinguished Cadet of his ROTC class. Mom and Mother Dubois attended the ceremony. I was the only enlisted man there in uniform, and I received the dollar for rending the first salute. I kept Pat's dollar until he was promoted to Full Colonel and, during the ceremony, I was granted permission to return the dollar to him.

Early in 1978, I was invited to attend an NCO Leadership Class graduation. A young airman assigned to TAWC wanted me there. After the ceremony, I was introduced to Colonel Dunwoody, Commander, 1st Special Operations Wing. He asked what I was doing. I told him how unhappy I was with my present assignment. He immediately called his personnel officer and requested that I be transferred to his wing. By the grace of God, it happened.

In March 1978, I began my final year in the Air Force working once again on aircraft and with NCOs and airmen. I was Maintenance Superintendent for the Wing. I had a great boss, Colonel Pinard. Together, we enjoyed fixing aircraft and building morale within the Maintenance group. *Thanks, Dad!*

After an excellent Operational Readiness Inspection and several major exercises, my career was coming to a close. What a finish! Colonel (General selectee) Dunwoody wanted me to be his senior enlisted advisor and requested that my career be extended three more years, but the request was denied at Tactical Air Command Headquarters. I was disappointed because I would have loved to stay on active duty for another three years. But Dad knows best. I spent the entire Christmas holiday writing and sending resumes to aircraft manufacturers. I received calls from McDonnell Douglass and Fairchild Republic. I went to both companies and received favorable results and offers.

I have not done the research but I venture to say that I am the first and most likely the last to be requested to sing at my own retirement ceremony. Colonel Dunwoody requested that I sing, *"Let There Be Peace on Earth"* during the Retreat Ceremony. Of course, I did. One of the letters read at my retirement was from General Lane, Inspector General for the Air Force. He wrote, "The Air Force is a better place to live and work as a result of the efforts of Chief Richardson and his family." Mom was there. The boy from Jackson Street had made a difference in the world's greatest Air Force because my Father in Heaven wanted me to.

Thirty years of life spent in a career should leave something for others to hold on to. I felt that I had done that. I entered the Air Force on a promise to help Dorothy financially to attend college. It is like starting off marching. When you start off on the right foot most likely you will be in step. The strong pillars of *Faith, Hope, and Love* supported me in times of trials. I faced stern and cruel discrimination, but remained focused because I had a promise to keep. I faced rejections but I stayed firm because I had overcome the difficult days as a youth, and I knew that to gain recognition would require fulfillment of the commitment to live in the *faith* that I had been taught.

I frequently reflected upon the words of my elementary teacher, Mrs. Lillie James, "Keep your bags packed because you never know when the door of opportunity will open." I knew there were rewards for doing things right. I had heard it from Reverend Johnson so many times during his sermons. The choir would support that by singing, *"He'll understand and say well done."*

The door has closed on those 30 years. The air power has grown, too. The old World War II aircraft have been replaced with supersonic aircraft such as the F-4, F-15, F-16, B-52, C-5 and the list goes on. The mechanics are better trained and the global challenge is still being met. And race relations are mightily and thankfully improved. *If I can help somebody, then my living shall not be in vain . . . Thanks Dad.*

Sgt Strickland my first white friend in the military Okinawa 1950

B-17 my first asignment as an aircraft mechanic Okinawa 1950

**Base Chapel Okinawa 1950 I sung my first solo
in the military during religious service**

**Singing the national Anthem opening the Bob
Hope show Fort Walton Beach, FL.**

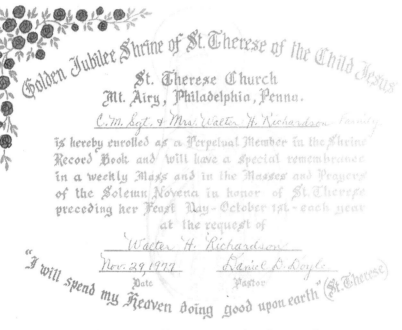

**Certificate enrollment into the shrine of St.
Therese of the Child Jesus 1977**

**Chito on the right. The child we sponsored
through high school and first year college**

Singing a charity concert with Edwena Feb 1983

Malamo store my first job after getting a bicycle for Christmas 1941

**Fr. Petter, after ten years ordination. We
became friends in the Philippines 1971**

Outstanding Airman banquet General Ryan and Secretary of Air Force 1972

**Lilly Ellen Richardson Devoux my mom
Feb 12, 1929 to Feb 12 1981**

**Greeting by General Okeefe and awarding
the outstanding airman ribbon 1972**

**Escorting Helen to the head table
outstanding airman banquet 1972**

**Singing group organized to entertain
the troops in Plieku Vietnem**

Superintindent largest propulsion branch in PACAF. Briefing SSgt Pearson admin Clerk

Baptizing infant at Hurlburt Field Chapel

407 North Davis Street where I was born

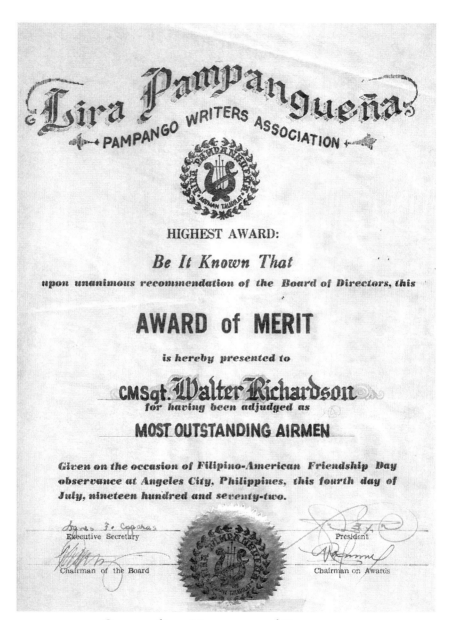

**Outstanding Airman award Pampango
writers Association, Philippines 1972**

General "Chappie" James and I during General
James recognition day in Pensacola, FL.

Organized at Dover Air Force base, Delaware 1963

Official Family photo to accompany outstanding airman nomination 1972

**Udorn Thailand 1974 - 1975 formed several
Cursillo weekends together**

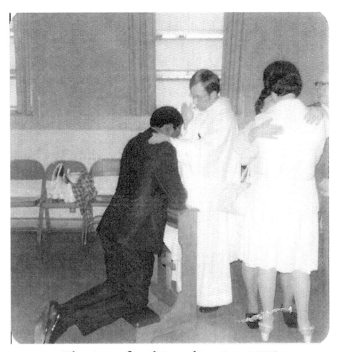

Blessing after his ordination 1975

First photo gift while attending Junior college 1952

To Chief Richardson and family
It is with great Pride and
honor that I forward this photo.
Please accept my sincere
Thanks for your strong support
+ guidance over the years.
The example set by you +
your wife paved the way for
the rest of us. I wish you +
yours the very best for the future!
God Bless
Gen Fig Newton

**General "Fig" Newton Commander AETC
friends since Clark AB P.I. 1970**

**Aircraft assigned to the technical school at
Johnson AB, Japan for training**

Band organized to entertain the troops in Plieku, Vietnam 1967

**Official photo acompanying the nomination
for outstanding airman of the year**

TITLE OF MILITARY AWARDS AND DECORATIONS, PROMOTIONS, AND DUTY ASSIGNMENTS OVER THE THIRTY YEAR CAREER
OF
WALTER HAROLD RICHARDSON
(The little boy off of Jackson Street, Pensacola, FL)

Arranged in order of importance
1. Bronze Star
2. Air Force Commendation Medal
3. Presidential Unit Citation
4. Air Force Outstanding Unit Award
5. Air Force Good Conduct Medal
6. Good Conduct Medal
7. Outstanding Airman of the year Ribbon
8. National Defense Service Medal
9. Vietnam Service Medal
10. Air Force Longevity Service Award Ribbon
11. USAF NCO PME Graduate Ribbon
12. Small Arms Expert Marksmanship Ribbon
13. Republic of Vietnam Campaign Medal
14. Army of Occupation Medal
15. Korean Service Medal
16. United Nations Service Medal

PROMOTIONS

1.	Private First Class	May 1949
2.	Corporal	June 1950
3.	Sergeant	December 1950
4.	Staff Sergeant	April 1952
5.	Technical Sergeant	December 1955
6.	Master Sergeant	May 1963
7.	Senior Master Sergeant	February 1967
8.	Chief Master Sergeant	September 1969

ASSIGNMENTS

1.	Lackland AFB, TX	January 1949
2.	Lockbourne AFB, OH	May 1949
3.	Okinawa	September 1949
4.	Johnson AB, Japan	December 1949
5.	Okinawa	April 1950
6.	Eglin AFB, FL	September 1951
7.	Itazuke, Japan	September 1957
8.	Dover AFB, Del	September 1961
9.	Pleiku, Vietnam	January 1967
10.	Dover, AFB, Del	January 1968
11.	Clark AB. PI	April 1969
12.	Griffiss AFB. NY	July 1973
13.	Udorn AB. Thailand	August 1974
14.	Eglin AFB, FL	September 1975
15.	Hurlburt FLD, FL	April 1978

Retirement January 1979

Ribbons

Wedding reception May 20, 1953

Rebecca

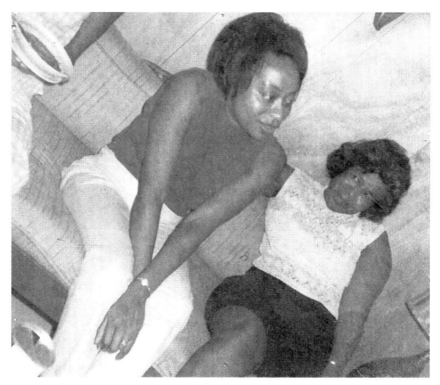

Dorothy with Another Person

Walt Richardson, Civilian

Precious Lord Take My Hand

The first morning of getting out of bed and not putting on the uniform was weird. It felt unreal that the years I had spent completing what would be demanded of me were behind me. My contributions as a member of the Armed Forces to a great nation had ended. I allowed my mind to drift back recollecting the places I had been and the people I had met. Those thoughts awakened a sense of pride that I had served my God and my country well. I had touched the lives of many people in and out of these United States and many miles from Jackson Street. Only my Father, God, knew how effective my efforts had been in meeting his Holy Will of *loving and forgiving* upon demand.

I continued to think that a whole lifetime from 19 years old to 49 – the prime of my life – had been voluntarily rendered to safeguard the freedom and security of our people. Too many of those people had never accepted me, a black man, as a full-fledged American citizen. Regardless, I asked myself if I would do it again and the answer was a resounding "yes," with the help of God.

As I slid off the bed to begin the start of the next leg of my life's journey, I prepared myself to go to St. Louis where I had been requested to come for a job interview. I did my usual daily ritual, attending Mass and remaining afterward to pray my rosary. McDonnell-Douglass and Fairchild Republic Company had expressed an interest in my *professional skills* obtained over a long career associated with aircraft systems and they wanted to discuss an opportunity of employment with them. At the interview in St. Louis, I was impressed with the interviewers and the corporate Human Relations staff. The interview went well. I returned home and immediately went to New York for the interview with Fairchild Republic Company. Again, the interview went well and both companies made offers.

Interviews over, I had to decide which company to choose. I put the question before my family as to where they would prefer to live. We had a hung jury. Three for St. Louis and three for New York, and Helen would not break the tie. That night after I finished reading my Bible, I wrote two notes, folded and placed them in the Bible. The next morning after Mass I asked the Lord to handle the drawing. I opened the Bible and the note I pulled was *"go to New York."* I did. *Precious Lord take my hand.*

Henri took time out of school to help with the driving to the Big Apple. Father Ariano had retired from the Air Force and was living on Long Island. After Mass on Sunday, he treated Henri and me to a Broadway show: *Eubie Blake.* This thrilled Henri because he had dreams of some day entertaining on Broadway.

I accepted the offer for a position as Maintenance Engineer at Fairchild Republic Company in Farmingdale, Long Island. The challenge was a great match for the work I had done during my 30-year Air Force career.

It was a new experience for me to look for a place to live. I had been living on military installations for so long; I really didn't know how to shop for living quarters. I received a call from a realtor and she was helpful. She introduced me to Mrs. Bullock who had just completed building a new home in Amityville. I agreed to pay the weekly amount Mrs. Bullock wanted. The location was great, only a few miles from where I worked and centrally located between two Catholic churches. *(One of my many homes, the houses of God.)*

Helen was unable to move with me because three of our children were in college. She was a social worker for Catholic Social Services and supervised the resettlement of the Vietnamese arriving in Fort Walton Beach, Florida. She found sponsors who helped Vietnamese families start new lives in their new homes.

At the end of May, I returned home to attend Donna and Henri's high school graduations. Donna was a cheerleader and Henri had won the talent contest: "Mister Striking Viking." Both were accepted to attend the local junior college. Lillie had moved to Tempe and was attending Arizona State University.

I chose to attend Mass at St. Martin of Tours in the city of Amityville. One evening while attending a concert, I met Mother Madera. She became a very close friend and I visited her home regularly. She enjoyed cooking and I enjoyed dining with her. I took her shopping and to other places she wanted to go. After knowing me and observing my outreach to others, she told me that my Christian demeanor had touched the lives of many people.

On the weekends, I assisted Father Ariano at the Catholic Chapel at Fort Totten. The facility housed military personnel assigned to West Point Academy and the United Nations. Sunday mornings after Mass, we had breakfast with Tom and Ruth Smith The faith community at Fort Totten openly welcomed me. I began to realize that I was a *professional freeloader.* I cannot recall turning down a single dining engagement.

I was in New York and attended the Mass that Pope John Paul II celebrated in Yankee Stadium. That was the largest attendance I had ever seen at a Mass. I learned that well-known people who were assisting during the Mass were Catholics.

Toward the end of the year, shortly after the Pope's visit, Archbishop Sheen passed away. I went to St. Patrick's Cathedral to pay my respects. I waited in line along with others for nearly an hour as mourners passed to view the remains. When I passed the coffin, I found a kneeler nearby and knelt to say my prayers. I had been there a little while when I was approached by a woman who wanted to know if I was the Cardinal from Africa. I responded in the negative, and she countered, "Are you sure?" I stood up and she said, "Perhaps not, because he is much shorter than you." She had attended the burial Mass, and the Cardinal from Africa had concelebrated the Mass with Cardinal Cook. So, she felt that I had denied my identity to prevent attracting people's attention away from Bishop Sheen's remains.

While I was home for the Christmas holidays, I was told by the Director of the Diaconate Formation Program that all of my transcripts had been forwarded to New York, Rockville Center Diocese, to complete my training.

After I returned to New York following my holiday trip, I made an appointment to visit the Rockville Center Diocese, Director of Deacon Formation Program to continue my training with his class.

When I arrived for the interview, the priest, the Director of Deacon Formation training had my transcript. He asked why I was in New York. I explained how I had accepted an offer to come there to work. He wanted to know why my family was not with me. I explained that three of our children were in college and were unable to move at this time. He wanted to know what kind of marriage I had. I explained that I had a good marriage; we were approaching 26 years. He said, "I will be straight forward with you. This program was designed for middle-class, Anglo-Saxons and I have no opening for you to enter this program." He gave me my papers and left the room. I went into the chapel and laid face down and cried. I had other things that had hurt me during the years but this was by far the worst. Later that Saturday, I visited Father Ariano and told him what had happened and his reply was that the church still had problems along racial lines. *My Dad, God, wanted me to become a Deacon.*

It wasn't long after I had been denied the chance to study with the prospective deacons of Rockville Center that my Bishop came to Brooklyn to talk about capital punishment, which he was totally against. I asked Father Ariano to go to Brooklyn with me to hear the Bishop's talk. During the reception after the talk, I introduced Father Ariano to my Bishop. He was aware of the problem I had encountered when trying to complete my Deacon's training. He turned to Father Ariano and asked if he would instruct me so that I would be able to be ordained that year with my class. Father Joe accepted gladly.

One day soon afterwards, while at work, I received a telephone call from my Bishop informing me that the Diaconate Committee had approved me to be ordained as a permanent Deacon. Once again, I cried, but this time for joy.

In May 1980, I returned home for our deacon's final retreat before ordination. I told the others about the lady who wanted to know if I was the Cardinal from Africa. At the reception after ordination, I received a gift from the other Deacons, a pair of red socks, and a plaque with the inscription, "Deacon *Cardinal* Walt Richardson.

My ordination was simply great. This was the first time both my Mom and my biological dad were at church together. Helen assisted me when the time came for me to be vested. Lt. Wayne Pat surprised me and arrived in time for the ceremony. My favorite aunt, Oshea, was there, too. Mother Madera, Pearl, Sister Virginette, Father Joe, and one other person came from New York to attend the celebration. During the reception, the Bishop handed out assignments, and he assigned me to the Office of Communications and gave me a scholarship, too, for Loyola University of New Orleans to attend an electronic media communications course.

During the private reception at my home, I received a telephone call expressing congratulations from Deacon David McNamara, Diocese of St. Petersburg. He wanted to know if I would accept an invitation to be guest Homilist at a very special Mass at St. Peter Claver Catholic Church. I accepted.

When I returned to New York, I was granted 30 days leave to study at Loyola University. I completed the course and began my work with the Office of Communications although I was still living and working in New York.

Some of the black Catholics knew about my ordination and asked if I would help form the Office of Black Catholics for the Rockville Center Diocese. I did. In order to help, I needed faculties. A letter was sent from my Bishop requesting that I be granted faculties to function as a deacon. Ironically, I was called in by the same priest who had rejected me earlier. He wanted to know who had ordained me. I answered that I had been ordained by my Bishop. He continued, "You totally disregarded my advice when I said that you were not fit to be a Deacon." He wanted to know what kind of Mickey Mouse program was going on in our Diocese. I did not answer. He wanted to know what I needed faculties for. I told him about the Office of Black Catholics which he denied ever knowing about and I was denied faculties.

I stood to excuse myself and offered my hand to thank him for his time. He refused to shake hands and said, "I haven't dismissed you, yet." I said, "I know, but its time for me to go." Again, I went into the church and cried. The priest wrote a letter to my Bishop stating that I refused faculties (in pencil no less). When I met with my Bishop, he said, "Just shake the dust off and carry on." I did. Sometime later I returned to

New York to serve as Deacon for the Office of Black Catholic Mass. I was the Deacon for Archbishop Moreno of Atlanta, Georgia. A person attending the Mass was aware of the problems I had encountered earlier with the priest and told me that he had *cracked up* on the altar. Law enforcement personnel had to come and take him out of the church. He was suffering all the time we were dealing with each other and I didn't know. . .*Sorry, Dad.*

Father Ariano formed a Cursillo weekend. I was the rector. I learned that Brother Nanny was on exile from the Philippines living with his daughter in New Jersey. I contacted and invited him to Long Island to help us. He came and was asked to talk during one of the meals. The candidates had heard about the Filipino gentleman I had embraced that night in the chapel. He told the other side of the story which I was unaware of. He said that the man I embraced was one of the leading lawyers in the Philippines. He had gone all over the country telling his story of that night when he was converted. . . *Something I didn't know, Dad.*

Fort Totten was not the only assignment Father Ariano was involved with. He was also associated with a school for dislocated boys, mostly from dysfunctional families. I helped giving lectures and singing when asked.

Mrs. Beatrice Bullock, the owner of the home where I was staying worked at a hospital on Long Island. She allowed me permission to use the kitchen and dining room. The living room had not been furnished. On Saturday morning after Mass, I would come and bake biscuits. She enjoyed them, but she had deep concerns about my openness. She was worried because most people were not as friendly as I was, and she thought that my southern hospitality would get me in trouble. Beatrice was divorced and she enjoyed talking with me and listening to my position on marriage and raising children.

She rented two other rooms, one to a young lady expecting a child. I came home after Mass one morning to fix breakfast and I offered the expectant mother something to eat. She accepted. While we were eating, she explained that the baby she was carrying had kept her awake most of the night. She continued, "When I get enough money, I am going to get rid of it." I said, "You don't really mean that do you?" She was clear about what she was going to do. I explained to her that God wanted that baby and if she just went through with it, He would take care of the rest. She became silent. The following weekend, Mrs. Bullock had breakfast with me and said I should not be feeding her. I explained about the baby and that she was planning an abortion. I wanted Beatrice to know that I would continue as long as I could to feed her and show love. I explained it was the condemned baby that I was feeding. Beatrice replied, "Only you would think like that." When I returned from Easter vacation, the young lady was moving out of her room. When I asked if I could help, she said, "Please, I am still bleeding from the abortion." I asked why was she moving and she said she was told to get out. I waited until Beatrice came home from work and wanted to know why she was putting the lady out. She said that she had entered Beatrice's room and had found a large amount of stolen money which she had used to have the abortion . . . *Sorry Dad, I tried.*

Soon, I joined the prayer group at St. Martin of Tours which met on Sunday nights. Sister Virginette attended, and we became friends. I was invited frequently to the convent to sing for them. It was at the convent that I met Father Ritter, who ran the covenant house for dislocated children in Manhattan. I was interested in his ministry of taking young prostitutes off the street and helping them to recover from drugs and getting them back to their families. I decided I should go downtown to see what was happening.

I took off on a Saturday afternoon and rode the train into town and I walked the streets alone. Approached by a kid carrying a boom box on his shoulder, I was thinking what I would do if I was asked for money. He came up and, guess what? He asked me for money. I retorted, "O lei dar sah dee wat." He persisted, "Man, give me some money." I continued, "O lei dar me sah dee wat." He said, "Man get off of it. You're black like me, you ain't no foreigner." He left. I went into a Burger King and sat down and began to laugh. I said to myself, "Lord, I don't know what I was saying but it worked." I continued to walk the streets and I saw more peep show stands and other activities and pimps offering girls. I made my way to St. Patrick's Cathedral and went in and prayed. "Lord, I am afraid. I don't want to go back that way." I heard a voice say, "Go back and don't be afraid." I did, and I was able to find the covenant house but did not enter. I went back, caught the train and returned to Amityville.

When I got home, Beatrice was waiting like a wet hen and asked where I had been. When I told her, she became very upset and so did Father Ariano. They both warned me never to do anything like that again. I obeyed.

Each morning when I arrived at St. Martin for Mass, I observed a woman dressed in black rushing across the parking lot. One morning I arrived just in time to be near her. I asked her name and she wanted to know why. I said I had watched her daily passing the church and going into the parking lot and feeding the birds. She told me her name was Hermes. I asked the members of the prayer group if they knew her. Someone replied that she was not all together, in other words, she was crazy. "Does anyone know her name?" I told them her name was Hermes and I thought what she was doing was good. They disagreed. In fact, the church wanted her to find another spot to feed her birds.

Before I was transferred from the company in New York to a smaller one in Crestview, Florida (to be closer to home because Mom had become very ill), I went to Mass and I didn't see Hermes. After Mass was over, I saw her digging in the dumpster across the parking lot so I went over to greet her. The birds were waiting to be fed. "Hermes, I missed you, where have you been? I wanted to say good-bye to you." She looked up and asked, "Will you lift the scarf from my head?" I did and I saw stitches. She was still wearing the hospital identification band on her arm. She said she had been struck by a vehicle while crossing the street getting food for the birds. I laid hands on her and prayed. I told her I had written an article and had sent it to the newspaper about how she was feeding the birds, but they never published it. She turned to me and proclaimed, "A prophet is without honor except in his own home." She embraced me and I said, "You are a good woman." I bid her farewell and God's Blessings.

My job at Farmingdale was interesting, considering it was my first time in industry after 30 years in the Air Force. I discovered that civilians did things differently, because I was unaware of the unions and the things I could not do if it was not in my task description.

I worked for a young lady who had limited knowledge about aircraft, but I helped her as much as I could and she was grateful. One day, I was called to the president's office. He was the General I had worked for while stationed in TAWC at Eglin before my retirement. He wanted to know what I wanted to do. I explained if I could be transferred to the Florida location it would help since my mother was not doing well. My Director of Logistics was once a Technical Representative at Eglin when I was head waiter there. He and I talked about the good ole days. I was only there for 18 months but so much happened during that time. I would ride for hours on the freeways enjoying the dinners I was invited to. I learned that I could write songs. While driving, I would get rip on a tune and later put the words to it. The first song was to St. Therese, the little flower.

In September, I was transferred to Crestview, Florida to become a technical writer on the engine test stand for the A-10 Aircraft.

As I look back, I discovered the purpose of my presence in certain places at certain times. It all involves the works of the Father, God. It was not meant for me to go to St. Louis; I would not have met the young lady I ministered to before her abortion. I would never have experienced the racial bias within my Catholic church, which I would help to remove. The following years would be lived under Holy Orders as a Permanent Deacon. *Thanks, dear God, for the calling and thanks, dear Lord, for holding my hands during the first year of my retirement.*

New World: New Mindset

A Closer Walk with Thee

Entering into private industry was so very much different from entering into the military. Military discipline was extremely helpful to me as I transitioned into civilian life. Addressing those in authority, using "sir" and "Mr. and Mrs.," were basic courtesy that I noticed were often disregarded when subordinates spoke to upper management. To me, it was a positive behavior I would continue.

In September 1980, I returned from New York to work in Crestview, Florida. Fairchild had a division there building sheet metal frames for a commuter aircraft. I was assigned as a technical writer for projects including modifications being made to the A-10 aircraft test stand.

Helen came to New York to help me move. She met the friends I had made over the 18 months. At a farewell luncheon, the company gave me a replica of the A-10 aircraft and a very nice mahogany shelf clock. Upper management told me, if things did not work out in Florida, I could return. I felt that this would probably be our last time together. Sister Virginette had us over to the convent for dinner before we departed. Mrs. Bullock had met Mr. Lockhart, and they were married before I left.

The Cursillo team gave us a farewell party. Father Ariano promised to come to Florida to continue our reunion started at Griffiss AFB. The main reason for the transfer was Mom's health. She had suffered a stroke.

(Helen had moved her into our home before the stroke occurred.) When I arrived back home from New York, she was in the hospital. It was so hard to see her unable to move about. She had been the pillar of strength for me over the years. I kept my emotions to myself, having done most of my crying prior to visiting her. She was in such bad condition the doctor treating her called me aside and said, "I know you are a praying man, so ask God to take her because all of the vital working parts in her body have shut down." I prayed for God to take her. After several weeks, she was moved from the hospital to a nursing home. She was there for only a couple of weeks, but it was long enough for me to compose a song in her honor. I went to the nursing home two nights before she passed away. I sang for her the song I had written entitled "*A Mother's Love.*" Early in the morning of my birthday, February 12, 1981, I received the call from the hospital that she had died. After crying for a while, I gave Helen the news. It had happened only three hours after Helen had left the hospital. I had class that night working on my degree in Resource Management at Troy University and had planned to go visit Mom because Helen said she didn't know how long she would last. I still didn't want to believe it. My very best friend had passed away.

A week earlier I had been invited by Mrs. Sanks to be the guest speaker for a black history program at Niceville High School. The Rainbow Ladies had planned the program. When I arrived at the school that morning, Mrs. Sanks greeted me, and I told her I would have to speak and leave immediately thereafter to go and make arrangements for my mother's burial. She apologized and offered her sympathy. She told me I could skip the program and go to Pensacola and take care of my business, but I insisted on speaking, ending the talk by singing the song that I had written for Mom.

All the family members were notified. I handled the arrangements with the funeral home and the church. The pastor allowed me permission to do the eulogy. At the end of my talk, I sang "*A Mother's Love.*" This was the most difficult thing I have ever had to do. The night during the wake, Father Thorsen assisted me in praying the rosary. Mom was one of the few (if any) Methodists to have the rosary prayed during the wake service. She had accepted a devotion to the Blessed Mother after her first stroke and miraculous recovery. Mother Dubois gave a portion of their family burial plot to Mom. Oshea, Mom's sister, took the loss very hard. The following day, I slipped away and went to be alone with Mom. This would be a common practice as the years went by.

The task that I was transferred to do at Crestview came to an end. The Plant Manager was quite pleased with my work and had come to appreciate my working there; he recommended that I fill a position that was about to open when the safety engineer retired. My safety experience from the years in the Air Force had paid off. I accepted the position, following which the facility enjoyed a long period with an outstanding safety record. Fairchild Industries', headquarters in Maryland, invited me to attend a safety conference in New York and speak about the safety program we had at Crestview. It was good returning to New York where I met my previous managers and had lunch with them in the plant lunchroom.

The timing for the safety conference was perfect. Father Ariano was the retreat master for the Archdiocese of New York, Military Ordinaries. The Archdiocese retreat house was located in New Jersey. Father had invited Helen and me to plan and stay with him in New Jersey when we came up to New York to attend the safety conference. We accepted, but when we arrived, he told us that there would be important visitors coming there during the upcoming week, and we could spend the first night at the retreat center but the following nights at a nearby motel where he had made arrangements for us. Father said he had a treat for us. He took us upstairs to the guest suite and explained that it was the room President Nixon had used when he visited that home, and he told Helen and me that we could sleep in the bed where the President had once slept. We did, and I don't remember resting any better in any other bed, but it was the thought of the boy from Jackson street sleeping in the bed previously used by the President of the United States that really made me humble.

Early that Monday morning, I left for New York to attend the safety conference. After the conference was over, I returned to New Jersey and, much to my surprise, I was asked to be Deacon for a Mass celebrated with the late Cardinal John O'Connor and two other bishops. They offered the Mass for Helen and me who were celebrating our 29th wedding anniversary that day. The Bishops were there preparing the Pastoral Letter on Peace and War, a very historical document reaching out to the Catholic Church in America and the world.

After the Mass, the Bishops had a cake for Helen and me to mark our anniversary.

We spent the week there and, on Saturday, we went on to Fort Totten to attend a wedding of one of the Smith's daughters where I sang the *"Ave Maria."*

When I returned to work at Crestview, a black gentleman stopped one day wanting to know about the cross I was wearing. I told him the cross I was wearing represented my status in the Catholic Church as an ordained Permanent Deacon. He looked surprised and said, *"I didn't know there were any black Catholics in this area."* I smiled and told him there were a few. Shortly after sharing with that gentleman, I was asked to come to Holy Name of Jesus Church and talk about the Sacraments to a Boy Scout troop. When I arrived to attend Mass, I caught sight of Mrs. Sanks whom I had not seen since leaving the school to attend to my mom's burial arrangements. She and her entire family were involved in helping during the Mass. I was so impressed because I had not seen any other black families in other parishes so involved.

After the Mass, Mrs. Sanks introduced me to her family. Her husband, Terry, and I instantly became friends. I made a suggestion. I told them about the black gentleman and how surprised he was to learn I was a Catholic. I went on to say that it would be good if we could do something during Black History Month to show that there were black Catholics in the area. This was the beginning of the longest running evangelizing effort in the diocese: **THE CATHOLIC AFRICAN-AMERICAN CULTURAL AWARENESS GROUP OF OKALOOSA COUNTY.**

All of this took place after my ordination. Immediately after I was ordained, I accepted an invitation to be the guest homilist for a special Mass at Saint Peter Claver Church in Tampa, Florida. This was my first invitation, and I would make every effort for it to be inspiring and effective. I really worked hard to prepare that homily. The Bishop welcomed me in the Diocese and had granted me faculties to preach that Sunday. Arriving the night before the big Mass, I was treated to a very nice dinner. That Sunday the church was overflowing with people. I read the gospel and entered into my homily. At the end I sang, *"How Great Thou Art."* When the Mass was over, I joined the Pastor and the Bishop at the rear of the church to exchange greetings with the people. A lady came up to me and asked if I was the man who had just preached. When I responded affirmatively, she said, *"Well, that was the worst sermon I have ever heard."* I was stung. Then a gentleman standing near-by heard what the lady had said and came over to me and confided, "Deacon Richardson, you don't know that lady but we all know she has a bad habit of repeating everything she hears others say. *"Amazing Grace."*

I was one of the first Deacons to be assigned to St. Mary. It was a different feeling from the first time I had attended Mass there 23 years earlier. I came into the assignment with the strong urge to evangelize more blacks to become Catholics.

During that weekend in Tampa, I met Mr. Francis Andry and Mrs. Beatrice Carter; they were invited to attend the Mass at which I preached and later spoke to the congregation about the Knights of Peter Claver. Their talk inspired me to join and become a member. The Knights of Peter Claver were formed by devout black Catholic gentlemen who were not allowed to join the Knights of Columbus. After meeting Mr. Andry, a great friendship developed and I became a frequent guest speaker at his parish in Chasting, Alabama. *"Amazing Grace"*

Near Reverend Woods' house was Nick's Nightclub. The building and homes close by had changed significantly for the better since I had first visited there in the summer of 1948. Close to the club was a giant oak tree where black men would gather during the weekend to drink whiskey and beer. I figured if I could get their attention I would have a jump start on my evangelization effort since I passed that tree and the group under it every Sunday morning on my way to sit with Reverend Woods while his wife went shopping.

I stopped one Sunday morning not knowing what to do or how to do it, but I did it. I greeted the men and told them that I was on my way to church and, just imagine, if I were going out of town to a place where you know someone you would want me to take a greeting for you, wouldn't you? Well it is the same thing here; I am going to church and if any of you would like for me to pray for you, I will. One by one they said, "Please say one for me." I left. I was nervous because I had not really told them the truth. I had already gone to church but I considered that as an icebreaker. So, the next Sunday I stopped again, and I apologized for the way I had come up and asked if they wanted me to pray for them. I thought about it and said, "You know I should have prayed right here." So I did. We bowed our heads and I offered a prayer and we all said *"amen."* I left. I felt much better that time, and I told Reverend Woods what I had done. The next Sunday I stopped and greeted the men and said, "Gentlemen, I want to apologize again. I have come here three Sundays and I have never told you who I am." One gentleman stated, "Mr. Richardson, we enjoy you coming by but if you really want to help, please see if you can visit our young black men in the county jail." I took his advice and the following week made contact with the county jail officials, and they arranged for me to conduct services there on Wednesday nights for the inmates. Since I was working in Crestview, this was great. I would leave work and go to the jail and conduct my services. *"Through many dangers toils and snares I have already come, twas grace that brought me safe thus far and grace will lead me on."*

My ministry began to blossom, and I was requested to do baptisms, witness marriages, preach during the Mass and take communion to the shut-ins. My singing was in demand and I performed concerts for different fund raising efforts. In May 1983, I earned my degree in resource management. That same year in February, I accepted an offer to work for RCA in a range-support contract at Eglin as a Safety Specialist. Fairchild Industries asked Management at Crestview to double the offer made by RCA to keep me on but the personnel officer decided not to, so I left a well-organized safety program. RCA was a great company to have on one's resume.

When I graduated from Troy State University, my supervisor challenged me to go for my Masters Degree, and I did. In August 1986, I earned my MBA. I was promoted to resource manager, and I recruited for RCA at different universities such as Mississippi State, University of Alabama, University of Florida, University of Southern Alabama and Tuskegee University. I was in search of Computer Science graduates and Electronic Engineers. During those trips, I was always able to find my Father's house. I found it to be a challenge to locate a Catholic church and attend Mass in the different cities I visited.

In May 1981, Lillie graduated from Arizona State University. We loaded our station wagon and took off from Florida driving to Arizona. Carmen was the oldest at home. Henri, Donna, Bill, Carl and Bitsy, the poodle, were all cramped into that loaded station wagon for the long journey. Still working for Fairchild at the time, I had to attend to company business at Kelly Air Force Base, San Antonio, Texas. It was a great stop because my aunt, Lucille, lived in San Antonio and had plenty of rooms to accommodate our family. Traveling across country was much better now because motels all across the country were accepting black people. We spent the night in El Paso, Texas and the following day we made it into Tempe, Arizona.. It was a great feeling to have our third child graduating from college. We enjoyed listening to Walt's Band, which had grown in popularity.

After the two-week vacation was over, we started our return trip home. We attended Mass at Tucson, Arizona. After breakfast, I took the car to the service station to get gas. The mechanic noticed a leak under the hood and asked how far I was planning on traveling. I said, "Florida." He said I would have to replace the water pump. I arranged for the family to stay in guest quarters at the Air Force Base while waiting for the water pump to be replaced. It was Sunday, and I was not at all sure that the mechanic would be able to get a replacement pump, but he did. While he was changing the pump, we talked. He told me about his wife's illness. She had had surgery to remove cancer from her body. I promised to pray for her recovery, paid for the repairs, picked up the family and started our trip home. We had gone only about 30 miles east of Tucson on I-10 when steam came pouring out from under the hood. I parked the car on the side of the road and flagged down someone to help. A car stopped and the gentleman asked if he could help. I asked if he would stop at the next town and send a wrecker to tow us back in. He did, and a mechanic came from Benson, Arizona. He escorted us into town and to the service station where he worked. It was near dark, and we had to find a motel near the service station.

Next morning we went to the service station. Inside was a restaurant, and we ate breakfast. The mechanic told me the car was fixed, but when I took it for a test run, it started steaming all over again. When I returned, he suggested that I call the first mechanic who had worked on the car. When I reached him, the mechanic apologized and told me he had failed to install the pressure plate behind the water pump, and that he would bring it to Benson. When he arrived, he paid the second mechanic and refunded us the money we had spent for the motel.

That was a really nice Christian gesture. I asked about his wife and he thanked me and said she was doing quite well. Late that Monday evening we resumed our return trip home uneventfully. Carmen had finished Junior College and was off to Florida State University. Henri and Donna were attending Junior College.

The safety program I organized for RCA gained recognition from the National Safety Council for working over one million hours without a lost-time injury. The Armament Test Center Safety Office also rated the RCA safety program "outstanding." Colonel Ed Hubbard, the Base Safety Officer, presented the company the Outstanding Safety Award. The National Safety Council award continued to be awarded to us for three years.

The jail ministry was really going well. Initially, I was granted 30 minutes to conduct the services and leave. After several months, I was asked to stay as long as I needed. There were times when front office staff members would ask if I would stay longer to meet with them. We always laid hands on the inmates who would be appearing before the judge that week. At the end of the service, the inmates would ask me to step inside the circle, and they would lay hands on me and pray. I am still receiving blessings from those prayers. The program grew. I was asked to include the female inmates. I arranged it that the men would come one week and the females, the next, and this continued until I left the ministry. The female deputy escort for the females asked if she could take instructions to become Catholic. I would stay after the services and give her instructions. I was so grateful when she asked me to be her Godfather during her baptism. I did. *"Amazing Grace."*

A female inmate was seriously affected by my preaching when I spoke of hope and how much they were loved. I would share with them how good it would be to talk with God. I encouraged them to build their faith and to offer their love to a God who would love them unconditionally in return. On the evening the females were to attend my services, you could hear them singing as they came from their cells, *"One day at a time, Lord."*

On a Saturday evening, I received a call from the Fort Walton Beach emergency room; the nurse wanted to know if I was Deacon Richardson. She asked me to come to the emergency room. When I arrived, I discovered that it was the female inmate who had really enjoyed my talks who was recovering from an overdose and an attempt to take her life. She had requested that I come to the hospital. She was conscious when I arrived. I held her hand and prayed with her. After she fully recovered, she never missed an opportunity to call and talk with me. Later, she fell in love, got married and the last I heard from her, they were doing fine.

My prison ministry ended in 1987 when RCA lost the contract at Eglin. RCA offered me a promotion and sent me to an assignment in the Bahamas.

In 1987, Bill graduated from Florida State University with a degree in dietetics. A walk-on for the football team, he ended up playing strong safety for the Seminoles for two years. At the same time, Donna had completed Junior College and joined Bill at Florida State where she was selected to be a cheerleader. Helen and I had the pleasure of meeting Bobby Bowden. I had never attended so many college football games. Bill made "player of the week" and really enjoyed playing. That same year in May, Lillie earned her Master's Degree in drama at Arizona University and Carmen earned her B.S. in recreation. Granny Dubois made the trip west with Helen and me. Once again, we enjoyed Rick's music. Whenever I am where he is entertaining, he requests that I come on stage and sing a number with his band.

Before leaving for the graduation, Helen and I attended Father Holley's ordination. He was the first African American to be ordained a priest for the diocese of Pensacola-Tallahassee.

When we returned from Arizona, I had to report to my new assignment on Andros Island, Bahamas. I became the Atlantic Underwater Test and Evaluation Center's safety administrator. This would become my greatest professional challenge because the island had a very relaxed attitude with regards to safety. At one point I had concluded this was not the assignment for me because I was unable to get management to take safety seriously. The Workmen's Compensation costs were outrageous. The Workmen's Compensation Insurance reserves exceeded $1.2 million. When I finally got the project manager's support, I called for safety training for managers and requested the attendance from General Electric Corporation. I invited Colonel Ed Hubbard, the Safety Officer from Eglin to come and assist in the training effort. Ed was a POW survivor. He came and spent two days along with the GE safety professionals. This was the beginning of a revised safety program. The Navy welcomed the new approach and the safety program began to gain special recognition from our Navy customers. The accident rate declined to its lowest point ever. The Workmen's Compensation costs declined from $1.2 million to less than $200,000. I received a nice reward for my efforts.

The Bishop of Nassau granted me faculties to function as a Deacon since he did not have a priest for the island. I started having daily communion services each evening at 5:30 PM. I had no one attend there until Helen moved to the island. On Holy Days, I would get other Catholics to attend the service.

I was attending a Hazardous Waste Management course in Virginia when I asked the priest on base if he had an extra tabernacle. He did. He gave me the one stored in the attic of the church. I had the lock repaired and brought it back to Andros. I had a roll-away stand made to secure the sacred host when Mass and communion services were over. The Archdiocese of Military Services granted me faculties to conduct services on the Navy facility. I organized a CCD program, conducted baptism training and announced that I was available for counseling. Father Howard was assigned to Fresh Creek, the city adjoining the Navy facility, where he became the contract priest. I assisted Father Howard on Sundays. He said Mass in at least six churches weekly.

My job was going well. I trained workers to wear the respirator, confined space, and on the use of personal protective equipment. I also worked out of my field in tracking hazardous waste. The contract required sea vessels to recover targets after underwater testing. As the safety program took control, the morale improved. I included the Bahamian workers in the program when, prior to my assignment, they were left out.

When Helen arrived, she accepted work at the "on-facility" school as head librarian. The best part of that assignment was free meals, free living quarters and tax-free income. GE had a private airplane traveling twice a day between West Palm Beach and Andros Island. Often we went to West Palm Beach to shop.

Prior to Christmas, I was asked to organize entertainment for the holidays. I invited my friend, Mike Mancini and his band, and they came over and did a great job. Of course, I had a chance to sing with them.

The Archdiocese Military Services heard good things about the limited Catholic programs I was conducting and sent Monsignor Ariano over to pass out letters of appreciation. At the end of my third year, I was asked if I would accept a position as Manager, Environmental Safety and Health in Colorado Springs, Colorado, and I accepted. During my tour at Andros, Lillie and Chris had come over to visit. Lillie had to stay back a few days because she was filming a part in *"Young Riders,"* playing a part with Della Reese. She explained how excited she was to meet the star. When she arrived, I was asked to share a few moments with her and Chris. They announced that they wanted to get married. Chris asked for my permission to marry Lillie, and I gave my approval.

In November 1998, Carmen called the island and told her mother that she was pregnant. When we arrived back home for Christmas, Carmen explained everything to us. I took time and visited with the suspected dad. I did not express any anger. I wanted to know what had happened since he was already married. He explained, but for some reason, whatever he said did not register. I let him go and accepted it for what it was worth. The incident resulted in negative affects on his marriage, which ended in a divorce. Still, I remained a friend to him. In discussing what I felt about the situation, I asked the others to leave this to God and to open our hearts to forgive. I wanted Carmen to know that we loved her and prayed that she would carry through with the pregnancy. Prior to our return home, Carmen had talked with Father Holley who was assigned to St. Mary after his ordination. He told her to accept her baby and let God do the rest. She followed his advice over what some others had recommended: an abortion.

In June 1999, our first grandchild was born. Helen and I arranged a trip home and were able to get back before Carmen and the baby were discharged from the hospital. Maureen, a very close friend of Carmen's stayed with her all during the delivery. On the day that Carl Joseph was born, I included him in my daily prayers, along with the other children and family members. I thought about my own birth and how Mom had wanted me so badly, she had withstood all criticism to accept God's will. No one really enjoys seeing a child entering the world with a handicap with regards to what society claims is an ordinary parenthood. Yet, time and time again, God selects the time and the situation to create a life. I was later told by a bishop to accept God's will and His way of bringing life into this world. He cited that the Blessed Mother was unwed when she conceived her son through the power of the Holy Spirit. Christians world-over know how St. Joseph willingly accepted Mary into his home and honored her desire to forever remain a virgin. I felt a great burst of love and then joy knowing that one of my daughters would accept God's will and bring into this world one who has turned out to be a great person and athlete.

At the end of my assignment at Andros, the project manager asked me if I really wanted to leave. He had come to really appreciate the safety program we had developed there. We had exceeded the National Safety Council job-related injury annual reduction ratio which is set at 3.0. Our facility was enjoying the lower percentage rating of 1.3. I must admit that I had more workers praying at the job site than I had in church. Every time someone would see my white vehicle roll up to their work area you could hear, *"O Lord, here comes Richardson."*

The challenges I had faced on my arrival, vanished. Managers called when there was a safety concern. I reviewed construction plans before the work began. I gave lectures at job sites. I conducted safety committee meetings. I enjoyed the naval comments expressing their appreciation of the safety program and the saving it meant to the government. But, it was time to move on. The local Bahamians were sorry to hear I was leaving for I had spent a great deal of time working with them after duty hours. The teenagers hated me when I first arrived because I demanded that they wear protective gear when riding on their skateboard ramp. I also restricted them from skating in the middle of the street. This should have been the responsibility of the parents, but they were allowed to do pretty much what they wanted to considering the sacrifice of living in such confined conditions.

Once, they had decided to challenge me, using their skateboards to go to the community dining hall. They occupied the whole street so I waited until they entered the dining hall, and I took all the skateboards to my office. When lunch was over, they had no skateboards. Some sent their parents to my office to get their skateboards, but I refused to release them until I had a firm commitment that the kids would follow the safety precautions I had instructed them to use. This incident of taking away their skateboards resulted in the organization of a skateboard safety committee. Together, we repaired the skateboard ramp and held shows to let them show off their skating skills. When they learned that I was leaving, they came to let me know how much they appreciated what I had done. I told them I did it because I loved them, that I would not have been able to handle the death of one of them from an automobile colliding with any one of them. They understood. *"Amazing Grace."*

Helen departed the island in November 1990. She went out to Arizona to prepare for Lillie's wedding. She had spent a month sewing for the wedding in the trailer we lived in on Andros. I was sent by GE Government Services to the Kwajalein Island to investigate a fatal injury that occurred on the facility. This gave Helen plenty of room and time to work on the wedding dress without me there to interfere. The dress was simply beautiful, and why wouldn't it be: Helen is a professional seamstress.

The entire family came to Tempe to attend Lillie's wedding. Bill and Edie who had married in November, Pat and Amalia who married a few days before Lillie and Chris in El Salvador; Henri, Donna, Carl and Little Carl, who was 18 months old, and also had a part to play in the wedding which he never did. Monsignor Ariano came from Washington, DC to perform the wedding. I was asked to assist as a Deacon. I sang before the wedding. Chris' family was there. We had a great time before the wedding and even more fun during the reception. Mother Dubois, Rebecca, and Bertha, my favorite cousin, rode out to Arizona with me. Aunt Rose came in from Chicago. Mary Dutko came from Orlando and took pictures of the complete ceremony.

Between Christmas and New Years, I flew to Colorado Springs for an interview for the position of Manager of Environmental, Safety, and Health for the Fort Carson Project. The project manager met with me and, following our talk, he made me an offer, which I accepted.

I returned to Andros after the Christmas holidays and started packing my belongings to move to Colorado Springs. Helen and I helped with the Martin Luther King program, which we held each year.

The years at Andros and involvement with the Catholic program gained special recognition from Bishop Ryan of the Military Archdiocese. He recommended me for the highest honor, a Catholic could receive the: "Illumi Christi Award." *"His eye is on the sparrow."*

The Twilight Years: Bright

He's More than Wonderful

Our trip from Florida to Colorado Springs was enjoyable. We spent a few days with Pat and Amalia. Alicia was in grade school. Pat was attending Command and Staff School at Fort Leavenworth, MO.

The promotion to manager was great. I was allowed to interview those interested in becoming my secretary. Millie was selected and together we developed an outstanding Environmental, Safety and Health program.

We were only there for a month when Helen had to return home and look after her mother. The house we were planning to buy had to be declined since I knew that I would have to stay there without my life's partner for my contract term of three years.

Managing the project's safety program kept us extremely busy as Millie and I developed safety-training programs and over the three years were successful in getting our employees the required training corresponding to their job classifications.

Besides being asked to help organize the Office of Black Catholics, I was asked by the Bishop of Colorado Springs to serve as Chaplain for the group. I assisted as Deacon at the post chapel and taught religious education to the high school students.

The Air Force Academy supported the Cursillo movement, allowing students to attend whenever possible. The commandant of the Air Force

Academy, who encouraged participation, was General Winfield Scott – the maintenance officer with whom I had worked when I was assigned to Itazuke, Japan. The Chaplain for the Air Force Academy was Colonel Father William Campbell, whom I had served with while stationed at Dover Air Force Base. Father Campbell was the one who had sponsored me for my fourth degree in the Knights of Columbus. It seemed as if I had come to a junction on my faith journey by encountering those devoted military leaders, and I was so proud to make it known to the Cursillo community that I knew those officers. It didn't hurt that the Bishop of Colorado Springs was also very active with the Cursillo movement.

Fort Carson appreciated the safety program we offered. A surprise Occupational Safety and Health Administration (OSHA) compliance officer appeared one morning at our facility. After presenting their credentials, he and his crew conducted an unannounced inspection of our company. I escorted them into the areas they wanted to inspect. We were fortunate in receiving only a very few minor criticisms that we were able to take care of without paying any penalties.

The office of Black Catholics invited me to attend the Second Black Catholic Congress held in New Orleans. I had attended the first one when it was revived in 1987.

General Electric was concerned about the money being paid out for job-related disabilities. The CEO authorized classes in key locations of the country, inviting all safety professionals to attend. I attended the one in Atlanta, Georgia, which gave me a chance to spend time with Donna who was living there. During Mass, I sang my usual "*How Great Thou Art*," and the reaction was overwhelming. The congregation stood for what seemed to be at least 10 minutes.

I returned to our project intending to implement what I had learned about managing disabilities. Our project was one of the locations where a very serious work-related accident had occurred before I had come on. The employee had been confined to a nursing home for over a year. When I met opposition from management, I wrote a letter to the CEO of General Electric citing what I considered a reasonable approach to get injured employees back to work. The suggestion was well received and communications went out from the CEO and much of what I had suggested was enacted.

With two tiers of my life completed (30 years with the Air Force and now over 10 years with private industry) I was thinking of doing something for myself. My Father, God had made life most productive and enjoyable, although day-to-day challenges were likewise always present, but I chose not to dwell on them. Constant reminders of unfortunate circumstances can *clog the wheels of progress*. I learned that it's impossible to plow straight ahead while at the same time looking back. The future is much clearer when looking ahead through the lens of forgiveness. This is what my Father, God, had taught me. *He's more than wonderful.*

As 1993 approached, I knew that the situation at home would not allow Helen to leave mother Dubois and return to Colorado, so I applied for retirement. In February of that year, I concluded my working relationship in private industry.

I returned home in time to attend our Black History Mass and I was assigned by the Bishop to be a Deacon for the military installation with service that would include all facets of my Diaconate ministry. I baptized babies, witnessed weddings, presided at wake services and grave side funerals. I assisted Marilyn Austin and the youth group. Visiting shut-ins and hospitals was most inspiring. It took a lot of courage to hold the hand of that first dying person. What an unusual feeling holding the hand as life drifts away. Then the agony that had once gripped the dying person would release and, at once, I could see the signs of peace. I knew then that the new life had begun. To be available to the family members at that moment is indescribable with the first reaction of grief and then the transfer of grief into acceptance. *Yes, My God is Real.*

While attending to my ministry, I felt the urge to become a safety consultant and accepted a position with McKinnie Construction in the company's safety awareness program. While attending to the company's safety needs, I was contacted by my former company to do a consultant job at the Kwajalein Island facility. For three months I assisted as safety consultant while the contract was being relinquished to another company. While there, I became involved with the missionary ministry. I was invited to attend a groundbreaking ceremony on one of the islands off from Roi De Moor. After Mass and the ceremony, I asked which priest was assigned to the island. The reply was that there was no priest assigned. It was explained that the people believed if they could build a church, God would send them a priest. Each morning during my stay at Roi De Moor, I would arise at four in the morning and walk for an hour.

Early on a Saturday morning while doing my usual walk around that beautiful island, I saw a light that caught my attention. When I stopped, I could hear a voice that I felt came from my Blessed Mother. She said she had long wanted the opportunity to tell me that it had been her desire to get help to my Mom when I was so sick at age four. She had asked her Son to heal me. It was at the hospital of His Most Sacred Heart that the healing took place. She said that she knew I would grow up and have a great devotion to her and share that devotion with others. As I continued my walk and praying my rosary, I experienced the most uplifting, inspiring feeling I had ever felt.

In 1994, I founded The Environmental Safety Awareness & Construction Limited Liability Company, providing training courses for safety management and environmental assessments.

During my annual physical, my medical provider discovered a small tumor in my prostate gland and the biopsy confirmed that I had prostate cancer. I notified my family and told them all what I had been told by the doctors. An appointment was made for me to meet with a surgeon at the University of Florida in Jacksonville who explained what would take place during the surgery. Arrangements were made to perform the operation in August, 1994. Before I went to the doctor, I attended Mass at St. Joseph's Catholic Church after which I remained to attend a weekly prayer group session. I asked for their prayers and told them I was in Jacksonville because of my prostate cancer. They laid hands on me and prayed. One of the prayer group members gave me a booklet with a 6-month novena to the Blessed Mother. The novena would end with a gathering at Caritas of Birmingham.

After I returned home from the doctor's visit, I started praying the prayers sent out by Caritas. As I was praying my rosary during my Saturday morning walk, the voice of the Blessed Mother instructed me to cancel my doctor's appointment and surgery and to go to Caritas in Birmingham. I returned home and told my family what had taken place during my walk. Under protest by my whole family, I called and cancelled my surgery and went to Caritas in December.

I called my dear friend, Father Hernandez, and told him what I was about to do. He told me to be sure and go to Caritas. He had visited there a year earlier so I went and I delivered his message and the community welcomed me. They allowed me to live with them in one of the trailers and I was assigned to the musician section. On Saturday, after I had finished my work, I went to the trailer to rest. One of the men living in the community came to my bed and said I was to bless myself for my illness. He gave me a pouch containing religious articles which had belonged to Saint Padre Pio, which I venerated. I blessed myself. I felt a warming sensation cover my body, and I was so relieved. I returned the articles and the gentleman left me alone. On the next day the priest who had pointed me out for the blessing, met with me and we had dinner together. He had been there all weekend but had never talked with me. He asked if I would be his Deacon at the final Mass held on the feast of *Our Lady of Guadalupe*. When the Mass was over, the retreat ended, too. I immediately called home and told them what had happened.

Later that month I went to my physician and I explained what had taken place. My doctor actually cried. She said, "I will still have to examine you," and she did, but she said to me that my prostate gland felt perfectly normal. I waited until the following year and returned to Caritas, this time to give thanks. I have gone over 12 years without any known problems. Regularly, I visit my doctor and do whatever I am instructed to do. *My Father is more than wonderful.*

Admittedly, my years in business have met many obstacles. I have faced severe financial problems. I have been sued three times. I have had to give up more than half my company to settle one of the lawsuits. All of those things only made me draw closer to my real father, God. The three pillars that supported me from my youth were still in place during those difficult months and years. God keeps the best secrets. No one knows what He will do. He sent me Juanita Sanks, and she became my office manager. Helen joined our effort and then my son, Carl. Then God sent me the opportunity to help build the Veteran's Clinic at Eglin Air Force Base. He selected one of the best construction companies in the area. Our efforts have paid off. The Veterans Administration has expressed its appreciation for the job we are doing with the hope of offering another project in the future.

One evening, I received a telephone call, and it was an invitation to attend the retiring ceremony for General Fig Newton. Many years had passed since we were stationed together in the Philippines. Helen and I went to San Antonio, Texas to attend the festivities. During his speech, he told about how this big, black chief master sergeant had taken him off to the side and had talked with him. He said he was told that if he listened, I would make him one of the best officers in the Air Force. He asked me to stand. Helen and I stood. The whole gathering gave us a standing ovation. As I stood, I heard someone scream. After the dinner was over, this lady ran up to me and hugged me so tightly and would not let go. She kept saying, "I never thought that I would see you again." Helen and I were held in suspense. She finally released me and told me that when we were stationed in the Philippines, I had come into her hospital room after she had been told she had a brain tumor and would be evacuated out for surgery. She said I cheered her up and sang to her. She said that I had given her courage and, since that time, she had undergone 10 other brain surgeries. She was there representing the Panama government as Ambassador-at-Large. The following day on Helen's birthday, she attended Mass with us and later treated us to a meal at the officer's club. A well-known artist, she gave Helen two autographed copies of her work.

I have passed my 78th birthday, have found peace in my heart, have raised my family. All of the children have attended college and are into their careers.

A few months ago, in 2007, I went to Jackson Street and took a picture of the house where I grew up. The Greek store next to the house is still standing but not in use. I went to my church and attended service. I knew only a few people there. I went past the side of the school house where Mrs. Lillie James taught, but only the steps are still there. Next, I went to St. Joseph where Helen and I got married, and I finally went to both graves: first, my Dad's grave in the National Cemetery and ended the trip at Mom's grave. Buried there were Mother Dubois who passed away after I returned from Colorado; my sister, Rebecca (who died just before Mother Dubois), and Jimmie, Rebecca's son. Pausing, I prayed and, during the reflection, it was reemphasized to me that I am the only survivor of Lilly's clan. I laid a rose on Mom's grave, prayed the 23rd Psalm and sang her favorite hymn: *What a Friend We Have in Jesus.*

When I returned home, I sat in the family room until the early morning hours letting my eyes wander over all the pictures on the wall, starting with our wedding picture; then my incredible Mom, Mother and Daddy Dubois, a portrait of all the family, which was sent to Washington along with the recommendation for my Outstanding Airman of the Year award. I looked at the grandchildren and my in-laws. Then I closed my eyes and prayed to my Father in thanksgiving for all that He has done for me. I must have fallen asleep. Soon, the morning sunrise was shining brightly through the large windows, and I thought, *Thank you, Dad for you are more than wonderful.* How Truly Great Thou Art.

Epilogue

TITLE	Writer
How Did he Turn Out?	H. Dann Wallis, Author <u>Burning Daylight</u>
To Whom It May Concern	Terrena Sanks, MEd Mental Health Counselor
Deacon Walter Richardson	Deacon John P. Morgan Past Vicar for Deacons Pensacola-Tallahassee Diocese

That Boy From Jackson Street

How Did He Turn Out?

I initially met Walter Richardson in 1996. I had come out of a boring retirement to become the Managing Director of Tec MEN (The Technology Coast Manufacturing and Engineering Network), and Walter as the President and CEO of Environmental Safety Awareness & Construction was a charter member. Tec MEN is a collaboration of 45 manufacturing and engineering companies in Northwest Florida who have formed the only successful cooperative network of its kind in Florida and one of a very few worldwide. At the time of that initial meeting, Walter, as an Associate Safety Professional, was making a presentation on workplace safety to the membership. During the presentation Walter stopped and asked a question about a point he had covered previously. . .offering a quarter to anyone with the correct answer. I had the correct response and Walter without breaking the continuity of his remarks, threw the quarter at me from across the meeting room. I never forgot that introduction!

Being new to my position, I was making appointments with each member to visit their company and seek their ideas about the Tec MEN organization. Most of those member meetings took about 30 minutes. That meeting with Walter took over 2 hours and culminated in lunch. At that time we were both into bar-b-que, but as our relationship matured over the years, so have our tastes and we've now moved on to

Chinese. Walter had a goodness and a peace about him that I found not only refreshing, but is often a rare commodity in a business leader and almost unheard of in a leader whose business was engaged in such a basic struggle for survival. I remember the first time I greeted Walter with the usual, "How are you?" He answered me then just as he does today, "I'm too blessed to be stressed." I quickly learned that with Walter it was not a clever response. . .it was an expression of his core belief! We thoroughly enjoyed each other's company and would engage in long talks about his life growing up and about his business problems; he would invite my business insights in response. Some days all I could give him was "just hang in there, it will get better." I don't know if I always believed that, but Walter's faith was sufficiently strong to carry us both forward. He is the first business leader I had ever been associated with who started each meeting with a prayer and gave thanks before each business lunch. I found it strange at first, but later in our relationship as crises began to appear in my own life, I would frequently ask him to pray for me . . . and he did . . . and they were answered. Fortunately for me, I was smart enough to hang on to a man with those kinds of connections!

One other unusual point about our relationship; being a former CEO now mostly in quiet retirement, I was just thrilled when the phone would even ring; often it would be Walter saying, "I need to talk to you, let's have lunch." Few people were calling to talk to me and none were inviting me to lunch. . .I was thrilled. In the time that followed, Walter became aware that I was doing some occasional management consulting work for four or five other local area companies. He asked me one day, "How come you never send me an invoice for your time?" I told him that was easy, "I don't charge my friends to have lunch with me!" He responded, "You are the only person with the understanding that I can discuss these problems with and you always share your thoughts and offer advice. That's consulting, and if you don't send me an invoice, I'm not going to call anymore!" So in the year 2000, I became an official consultant for ESA&C, and proudly remain so until this day. As my retirement time began to fill with other interesting and important things, I gradually backed out of my consulting practice. . .except for Walter. At a lunch one day Walter asked me if I was giving up consulting. "I am, but I won't quit ESA&C until you do." That was the wrong thing for me to say. . .Walter Richardson is a perpetual motion machine, he will never quit and thus, I will never get to either.

The more I became involved in his business, the more daunting and challenging the task appeared, for both of us. His company's major unit's primary business involved asbestos and lead abatement and clean up and each project required bonding. But because of the nature of the hazard and the small size of his business, bonding was almost impossible to find and if found, never at a reasonable rate. Most of the contracts being serviced by ESA&C were related to some branch of government. All levels of government, but especially the federal level, are notoriously slow payers. Thus, cash flow was always a problem and yet employees and suppliers expected to be paid in a timely manner with the accounts receivable problems belonging uniquely to the owner. Further, because of the profit history of the company, finding a loan with manageable terms was a major problem, even a simple loan to cover the government's period of payment float. Walter and Helen, their family members and friends all sacrificed and even mortgaged and second mortgaged their homes to keep the business solvent. . .but it was all gradually sinking. However, the most distressing aspect to me was not only the lack of support for Walter by some of his employees and partners, but their outright efforts to embrace and hasten the failure of the business. I did so want these people fired, and not only recommended it to Walter, but volunteered to do the deed! By contrast, Walter has lived his entire life by the *Golden Rule* and truly believes that at their core, everyone has redeeming qualities and we just needed to find and then appeal to those qualities. To his undying credit, Walter was true to his faith and made every attempt, far beyond that of most people, to make that appeal. . .to find those qualities. His generosity over the years of those relationships with promises made of their shared future and of ownership sharing would, in the end, come back to cost him considerably. But, it was a price Walter paid willingly to regain control of his company, but most importantly, to give to men who had not earned it, a jump start into their own business.

In 2004, the favorable publicity Walter and ESA&C received as the "Black Business of the Month" provided an opportunity for us to seek a more willing loan partner with a local banker. We set a meeting with the bank president and a loan officer in Walter's office. As the date for the meeting approached Walter asked me just how he should present the business to these bankers. I told him, "It's not the business that will make this deal, it's Walter Richardson. Don't even mention ESA&C, just tell them about Walter Richardson the man who started on Jackson Street and what makes him a good investment." True to his practice, Walter began the meeting with a prayer. He then made a brilliant, heartfelt presentation and brought all of us nearly to tears as he talked about that boy from Jackson Street. . .imagine that, a banker near tears. Then to cap the deal, Walter, who is a marvelous cook, presented his guests each with a homemade pie. A new loan arrangement was promised before they left the table. Truly, in 40 years in business, I had never been in such an unusual meeting and especially to have it turn out so successfully!

With the pressure of the near-term cash flow now eased for the moment, we began to talk about Walter's vision for Helen and himself, and their business; and most importantly, how we might get there. Longer range, Walter and I saw him, not as someone responsible for the day-to-day operations of keeping equipment busy, making weekly payroll for 16 employees, finding bonding and all of the hundreds of elements of running a business in now two hazardous business arenas. He wanted to move toward being able to use his well earned bidding deferments to pursue set-aside contracts with the government. The company's 8(a) status had reached its expiration, but he did have a 100% combat disability that would provide an occasional contract bidding advantage. What was needed to realize this vision was to offload the two existing business units, along with equipment, employees and responsibility for on-going contracts. In spite of the past relationships, Walter offered to set each of the two business managers up in his own business and move all of the elements to them and out from under the ESA&C umbrella. Considering all of the circumstances that had preceded that moment in their relationship, this was a most uncommonly generous offer! My recommended solution was considerably more drastic and final, but Walter's wisdom and loving heart would prevail. Before it was all finalized, the lawyers would also become large benefactors; I guess it is human nature when someone offers you an unearned and undeserved opportunity to try to reach for more. But Walter remained faithful to his long-range vision for the company and eventually the spin-off was accomplished.

In this vision for his new company, Walter would align himself with larger companies who possessed the wherewithal to complete larger contracts in the construction, demolition and abatement areas, and who would agree to become a subcontractor for ESA&C. Walter, in partnership with those selected companies, would bid on set-aside contracts that the larger partner could not qualify for. Essentially, Walter became the prime contractor and the contract manager. In addition, Walter would continue at a more leisurely pace in his core area of expertise to conduct training classes in the hazard abatement and safety areas. He would also continue to pursue Phase One environmental studies. He would be able to generate a positive cash flow with which to retire debts and maturing accounts payable, be more selective in the work he bid and the partners he would work with, prepare the company to pass to one of his children, and find more time to exercise his faith as a Deacon of the Catholic Church. Not that his service to his church ever suffered. I can remember at a time asking him which was his vocation and which was his avocation. He would remind me that doing the work of The Lord God was always our vocation! In all things, success now began to find the "Boy from Jackson Street."

This success could be no more apparent that his partnership with Lord & Sons to become the prime contractor for the $4 million contract to construct the new Veterans Administration Clinic on the grounds of Eglin Air Force base. Finally in the leadership of Lord & Sons, Walter has found a partner with the same core values and belief system as his. . .an unbeatable combination! But that is just not my opinion. At a recent on-site meeting to review the project completion status with our elected congressional representatives and appointed officials from the VA, it was announced that this beautiful, much needed facility, was UNDER BUDGET AND AHEAD OF SCHEDULE! When, pray tell, was the last time you heard either of these pronouncements used to describe a government project?

With encouragement from a lot of people who love him, Walter has elected to use some of his new leisure to write his memoirs. All should read them as his is such a compelling story of a man who never forget his early teachings, and never lost faith, even in the face of supreme adversity. I know of a contractor who has declared bankruptcy no less than 12 times. If ever a business leader had the opportunity and the reason to hide from such overwhelming debt and the piling on of business problems, it was Walter Richardson. The fact that he refused to do so and never ran from his responsibilities should tell you more about the character of this man that my meager efforts here ever could. I declare it my good fortune to have been associated with this man I proudly call, "My Brother" for these 12 years, and I am honored to have been allowed to express that in these words.

From their vantage point, Miss Lilly and Miss James can look down on this "Boy from Jackson Street" and give each other a "high five" knowing they did good. . .real good!

With great love and respect,

H. Dann Wallis

September 7, 2004

To Whom It May Concern:

This letter is intended to demonstrate my pledge of support for Mr. Richardson and Environmental Safety Awareness and Construction. Two words come to mind when thinking about Mr. Richardson: self-sacrificing and committed. Webster's dictionary defines dedication as "self-sacrificing" and commitment as: "The state or an instance of being obligated or emotionally impelled." When thinking about these words and what they mean to me, I have to look at the inspiration that surrounds me. Mr. Richardson is that inspiration.

Mr. Richardson has been a part of my life for the past 25 years, since age 9. I met this remarkable man through my parents, Terry and Juanita Sanks, while at a school function, who knew that the next 25 years would be an added blessing for my family and me. From age 9 to 19, I saw the friendship between my dad and Mr. Richardson grow and flourish. They had long talks about their children, the church, life, and their dreams. They shared their love of singing by forming a singing group – the Marion Singers. They performed in countless venues over the years, fulfilling one of their many dreams.

Both my father and Mr. Richardson were/are very spiritual men and they each had a touch of Martin Luther King Jr. in them. They both had a dream. This particular dream was to see a Black History Catholic Church Service, which would portray Black Catholics in church and their roles in the church. They wanted Okaloosa County to realize that "yes, Black Catholics do exist." These two men brought their families together along with other Black Catholics in the area and formed an African-American Cultural Awareness Group. This group raised funds and fought to have the service. They topped it off with inviting one of the 13 African-American Bishops in the U.S., and he came. This service continues to take place every year in February, and each year it continues to grow. Their dream was recognized, organized, conquered, and continues on to this day.

My father died in 1989 of cancer and at age 19. I never would have thought that anyone could come close to filling his shoes. As I got older and wiser, I realized that Mr. Richardson made a commitment to my father and promised that he would watch over my family. Mr. Richardson never tried to fill my father's shoes, but each time my family needed him, for whatever reason, Mr. Richardson kept his promise. When my brothers need advice, they go to him. He cheers them on and prays for them through all of their accomplishments. When my oldest brother switched careers and went from a USAF captain to a lawyer, he prayed for him. With each USAF military rank, he is there in support of my middle brother, the now lieutenant colonel; my youngest brother made it through West Point with the prayers of my mother and father, but the transition from being a captain and fighting in the Gulf War to family and civilian life were helped along by the prayers and conversations with Mr. Richardson. When I needed career advice, I went to him and the best advice he ever gave was telling me, "When you get what you prayed for, why question the blessing?" I still use those words when making my career decisions and life decisions. It was Mr. Richardson's way of letting me know that the Lord knows my prayers, even the ones I don't speak. When I seek guidance on life, I know that his door is always open, and I've used it on many occasions. In many cases, it is the "fatherly" advice that girls get from their fathers that he is gracious enough to give to me. When my mother began looking for a new career change and a good positive working environment, she went to work with him. This has been a two-fold blessing for both families. But for me, I don't have to worry about her because I know that she is going to be treated properly on the job, and that Mr. Richardson and his lovely wife will watch over her off the job as well.

Not only has he dedicated his life to his family and his spiritual growth, he remains dedicated to my father's friendship and last wishes as he has added my family to his family. Mr. Richardson continues to demonstrate his undying commitment and dedication to my family and me as he has done throughout the years. This exemplary display of unselfishness is a rare find in today's world and the Sanks family is grateful for it.

Thank you for taking the time to allow me to express my appreciation, commitment, and continued support to Mr. Richardson and Environmental Safety Awareness and Construction.

Sincerely,

Terrena M. Sanks

Terrena M. Sanks, MEd
Mental Health Counselor

Deacon Walter Richardson

My initial recollection of meeting Walter Richardson was at the first Cursillo ever held in the Diocese of Pensacola-Tallahassee. It was Men's Cursillo #1 at Eglin AFB near Fort Walton Beach, Florida. I had attended my own Cursillo only a few months before at Switzerland, Fl, and I was ready to help whatever way I could to share my faith with other men. There was the very tall black man who had a deep booming voice, a smile all over his face and always carried a Rosary wrapped in his left hand. He was so full of the Spirit and gregarious that I immediately liked, and was drawn to him. I am proud to say that we have been friends ever since, almost 30 years later.

This Cursillo was only one of many we participated in together over the years. He was the founder of the Cursillo Movement in our Diocese. The movement of which we were a part didn't stop with only men; it expanded to the women's movement as well. I am sure there are literally thousands upon thousands over the years whose lives have changed as a result of this action, which he started at Eglin AFB. It expanded from Fort Walton beach to Pensacola, Panama City and Tallahassee, all of which are in our Catholic diocese. He was ever ready to share his faith experiences with anyone who would listen. As he was an enlisted member of the Air Force, I was impressed with the stories of the many friends who were generals on down in rank. It seemed that his outgoing personality overshadowed any classifications that the military may have had. His commendations at work were many, although I can't comment on these specifically; he reached the highest enlisted rank of *chief master sergeant.*

When invited to his home, I observed his many children and wife. I noticed there was always music, laughter and love shared there. I never felt like a stranger when visiting. Both he and his wife Helen were always outgoing and proud of their family and were never judgmental. I am sure there were always those problems we have when raising a family, but it was never discussed outside of the family unit. The love shown always overshadowed all.

Unbeknown to each other, we applied for the Permanent diaconate at the same time when it was offered in our diocese. We were the first class ordained in 1980. I mention this because it only showed the extent of commitment he had to the Lord and his work. It involved four years of preparation and study and there was no remuneration of the material kind to be a deacon. Although work-related problems geographically for him crept in, he never wavered and sought out other ways to temporarily work out formation classes in another diocese and was ordained in 1980 with his Pensacola-Tallahassee classmates. I remember him coming to Pensacola on one occasion in the early evening and he took me with him to a "social club" to intercept a man who he thought had potential for the diaconate, but was misguided in his directions. The man with drink in hand, looked at us like we were crazy to be there. To make a long story short, this man did change and become one of our outstanding and respected deacons until the day he died at 70+ years. Walter, with his rosary in hand, frequently drove the 50 miles to Pensacola with a charitable mission in mind as I am sure he did elsewhere. Always holding and saying his rosary as he traveled, he told me once, "That the rosary was his car radar." Only God knows the good this man has done with his life and musical talent over the years; music and song were his vehicle for reaching out to all faiths and people, not only ours.

One of my many recollections was his devotion to St. Theresa of Lisieux. He always had faith in her and commended his prayers to her for protection of not only himself, but the family and friends for which he prayed. "She will shower down Rose petals of blessings on you," he would say. It has been an outstanding pleasure for me to know Walter over the years and to share his many experiences of faith. I can never pass up this one recollection: I was passing through Fort Walton early one morning and I called Walter's house and his wife Helen, still in bed, answered the telephone. She said he was in the shower but wait because he was almost out. Well, I waited, and waited, and waited, but no Walter. Finally I hung up and went my way. Later I found out from him she was still holding the phone – sound asleep – and he was wondering why?

Please call me if I can further expand on this short recollection I have written. I know there is much more but the one thing I can say with all honesty is: I am glad our paths have crossed in this life. My Catholic faith has grown and I am a better man as a result of knowing him.

Deacon John P. Morgan
4870 Livingston Drive
Pensacola, FL 32504
(850) 477-7296

August 10, 2007 – Feast of St. Lawrence

CHRISTIAN RECOGNITIONS

Baptized Christian	Feburary 1930 Allen Chapel AME Church
Youth Choir	Allen Chapel AME Church
Honored Sunday school attendance	Allen Chapel AME Church
Senior Usher board	Allen Chapel AME Church
Soloist	Chapel, Kadena. Okinawa
Baptized Catholic	June 1957
Vice President Holy Name Society	Itazuke AB, Japan
Confirmation	1958 Itazuke Japan
Cantor	1959 Itazuke
Soloist	Chapel Dover AFB, Del
President Holy Name Society	Dover AFB, Del
3rd degree Knight of Columbus	1962 Dover Del.
4th degree Knight of Columbus	1966 Dover Del
Lecturer	Chapel Dover Del
Soloist	Chapel Pleiku Vietnam
Eucharistic Minister	Clark AB, PI
Lay Cursillo Leader	Diocese Pensacola-Tallahassee
Ordained Deacon	May 1980
3rd degree Knight of Peter Claver	June 1983
Nominee Lummi Christi Award	February 1991

CPSIA information can be obtained at www.ICGtesting.com
Printed in the USA
LVOW06s1108090414

380996LV00001B/69/P